ESCAPE FROM THE GLUE FACTORY

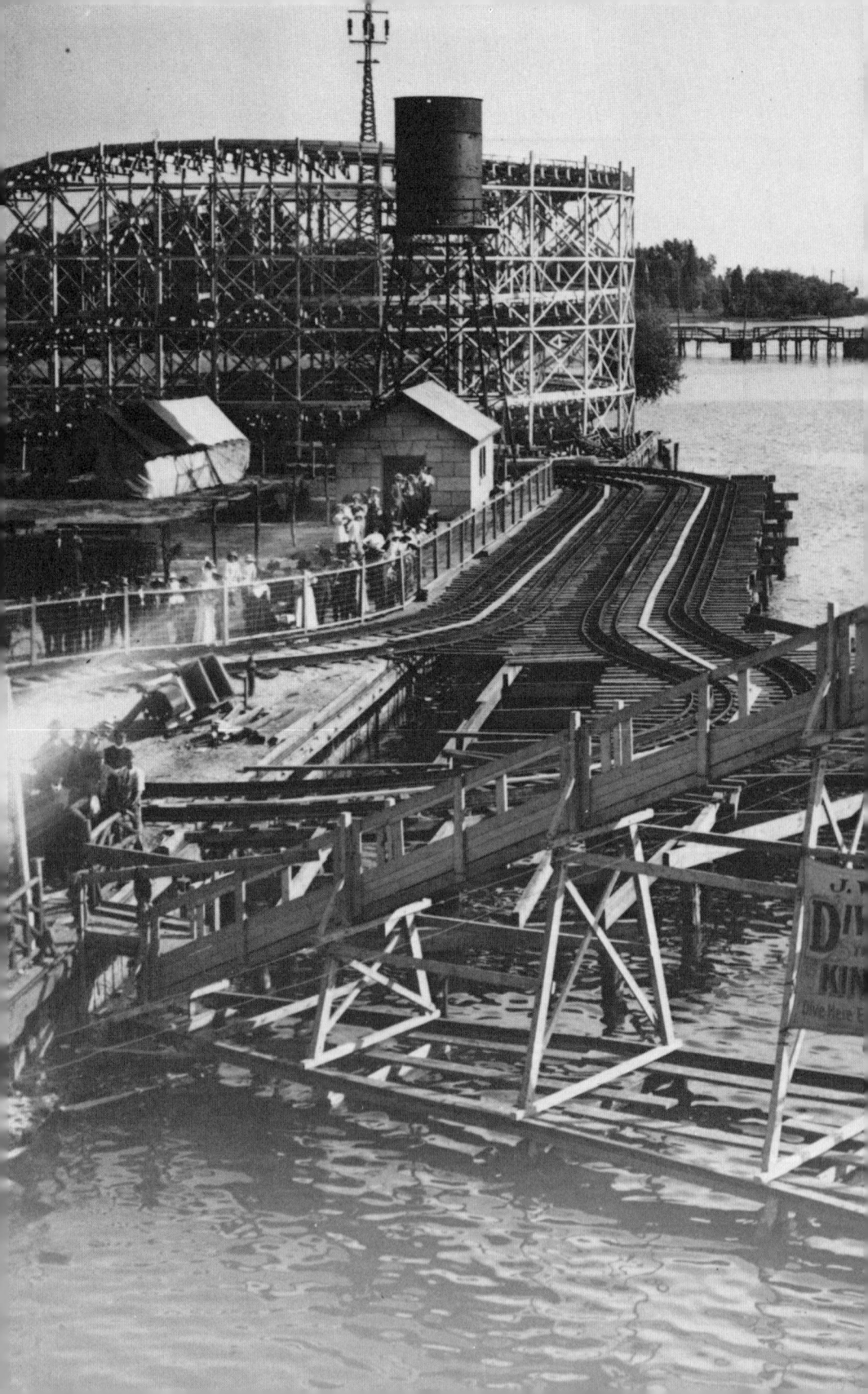

Joe Rosenblatt

ESCAPE FROM THE GLUE FACTORY

A Memoir of a
Paranormal
Toronto Childhood
in the Late Forties

TORONTO
Exile Editions

Copyright © Exile Editions Ltd., 1985
Reprinted 1987

This edition is published by Exile Editions Ltd.,
69 Sullivan Street, Toronto, Canada.
Exile Editions are distributed in Canada and the United States by
Firefly Books,
3520 Pharmacy Avenue, Unit 1C,
Scarborough, Ontario
M1W 2T8

Typeset in Stempel Garamond *by* Tumax Typesetting Company Ltd.
Designed by Lou Luciani
ISBN 0-920428-72-X

Special thanks to the city of
Toronto Archives for the photographs,
Diving Horse 1905 and *Civic Abattoir* 1910.

Drawing entitled '*Escape from
the Glue Factory*,' by the author.

*To all the monsters in my life
who made me who I am.
I thank them for it.*

Contents

My Shrine by Numbers	1
Blossoms in the Shrine	3
Deep Fried Dream	5
The Meditation Tanks	8
Birth of a Liberal: 1947, 1948	16
"A Chinaman Can Do It"	21
Manny	23
Magic Voyeurism	24
Scott	27
The Vampire	29
The Invisible Line	33
When Monsters Smoked	36
"Yank ... You Talk ... No?"	42
Mummies & More	43
The Friendly Giant	49
On the Street of Dreams	51
Pea-Brained	53
Horse Meat	55
A Few Hors D'Oeuvres	62
Survival	65
City Wild Life: Ants, Bugs, Bread Mould, or the Heat of '48	71
"And I Thought You Were Selling Knowledge"	75
Experiments in Mood Food	79
Pike the Milkman	81
Miss Blossoms	83
Miss Pettybones	85

Glue, the Serpent, and Lunch	87
Eddy in the Ice	91
The Meat Freezer	92
Miss Orchard	93
The Lake	96
Moose Call: On a Tree Frog is a Unit of the Universe	99
Dream Frost	104
Time in the Buff	105
In His Bandages, The Poet	111

My Shrine by Numbers

My mind roves sluggishly, then slices through birth water, propelled like a channel catfish, searching for the house where I was *bar mitzvahed*, that sanctified front room with its high pale green ceiling, a room on a tree-lined street, rows of embracing chestnut trees, and it seems like aeons since I was *bar mitzvahed*, a gray spot on the winding sheet of memory ...

The building on D'Arcy Street has vanished, gone like a shy creature into the fog. Some malignant force has nudged the house down the block or ripped it out, leaving a cavity, a parking lot in its place. The D'Arcy Street Talmud Torah is gone, and so, I'm sure, is rebbe Noble. The neighbourhood has borne the strain of time, even the chestnut trees seem bent. I remember those trees when they were young, ragged and wild, the spikey green capsules falling, striking the sidewalk, cracking, the white flesh inside exposing a dark brown eye, and hundreds of those empty green shells torn apart by wind and rain ... brown eyes strewn on the lawn.

The chestnut trees spread over the lead-painted dwellings, proliferous leaves. Like some senior elephant, my shrine wore a russet skin and inside dwelt a plebein Hebrew soul: ragged yellow wallpaper bubbling here and there from anxiety, the oak veneer floors covered by an inexpensive tile, in which an aquamarine floral arrangement swam against a creamy background, blending into a seeded gold and silver inlay ... asterisks glistened and had a quieting effect. I studied the rhythms of the surface of the tile ... eye allerted to the various gravities, hot and cold zones ... The tile had a will of its own and a penchant for stealing footprints from worshippers during winter.

I love an aging house, plasterboard showing through the chipped paint, a dwelling older than Noble, its ribs revealing the seamier side of growing old, paint applied to paint, unable to hide decaying liverwarts, an aged heart barely alive under freshly painted skin.

There was a mural in the tiny vestibule, a mural that seemed to have been painted by numbers. A pencilled outline had been left on the wall. Trees pencilled-in had been partially erased, but the perimeters had been left. The mural complemented the tile, giving off a sallow light and an odour of stale oil paint and turpentine ... the usual forest scene ... derived from European wall hangings ... the shaft of sickly yellow light ... dabs of ultra-golden sunlight ... exaggerated light-beams on a mushroom ... and there, the familiar puzzled stag without testicles. Done by numbers ... a wilderness painting and this de-gendered creature in the landscape, in a patch of toadstools, lost, licked and sucked by a mouth of bad lighting. The picture cried out for an androgynous youth ...

But wait: a brown moth is trying to dominate one area of this world of numbers. Did the painter stop and let his assistant continue? A brown moth resting in vigorous sunlight, a moth with a real stomach, who dominated and had intensity ... leaving a shadow, a surrounding blurr ... Outside my shrine, green spikey planets fell from chestnut trees, splitting on the pavement, exposing their brown eyes.

Blossoms in the Shrine

If I could number my memories I'd paint myself into a corner. There wouldn't be enough good bourbon to wash the sadness of the brushes. Still, I remember a sweet time: one Fall afternoon, when pain finally realized its bar mitzvah blossoms. Following the ceremony held at a store-front synagogue down the street from the D'Arcy Street Talmud Torah, guests marched down the hall to the back of the house into a makeshift banquet hall and seated themselves at their designated banquet tables. Rebbe Noble, an inscrutable septuagenarian, banged a drinking glass to get everybody's attention, and soon his absolute authority held the whole room silent. He lauded the bar mitzvah boy, intelligence ... drive ... and announced I was about to make a speech, in Yiddish.

I praised my beaming parents, my uncle sitting silently nearby, and rebbe Noble for his tireless instruction. Then, I ended my speech by thanking the assembled guests for attending my confirmation, wishing them a good appetite, which was a cue for the kitchen staff to get the machinery in motion.

Thunderous applause ripped through the hall. A few among the hard-pressed volunteer kitchen staff ventured out to contribute glee. The women, my mother and friends, had prepared geflite fish and laid out hundreds of evenly roasted capon parts cooked in their own wild juices. Chicken parts faced lilliputian Prince Edward Island virginal spuds. My attention was glued to salient islands of chicken ... tall thighs and legs bejewelled by their own frizzled grease, authentic Chicken, not birds fertilized by artificial light. The food was heaped onto huge serving plates accompanied by trays of baked egg bread, the twisted *chalah*, freshly glazed, braided, lightly tanned.

The guests were overwhelmed as I was: this was the first course. It beamed on me that perhaps the guests had tolerated my youthful exuberance out of civility. The dollies arrived loaded with mounds of steaming food: an aromatic tide swept the banquet room; kreplech, chopped liver, chopped raw onion, herring in its skin of schmaltz, bowls of cabbage soup, cold beet borsch, more plates of chopped onions, eggs, as a gastric seismograph recorded the ebb and flow of stomach acid, playing a glyphic arrangement on the mind, and my palate, abstracting itself, became a wolf eel lusting after kishka, an intestine stuffed with onion, flour, seasoning, and roasted to a deeply hued brown. This was no ordinary intestine, but one taken from a bovine of delight.

Rebbe Noble clinked his glass. He proposed a toast to my folks ... uncle Nathan ... the janitor ... the cooks in the kitchen, whose names he had memorized so as not to offend, and before he tossed down a tumbler of schnaps, mumbled a blessing. Then the bread was blessed and appetizers leading to the main course. I marveled at the rebbe's alcoholic tolerance.

Nobody poured a shot for me. I had, after all, become a man and had earned the right to a drink. The good rebbe turned down my request before I could even ask for a drink. His eyes sparkled and he laughed softly into his shot glass. Turning aside, I saw a private table dominated by an élite of gray beards who waved me away from their zone of influence, segregated from the others, a gerontocracy unto themselves. "Go Vey ... *gey avek*," they shouted in Yiddish and chopped English.

I was not to be denied firewater. I swiped a bottle of Canadian Club and in the privacy of my room at home drank it quietly, trying to outdrink rebbe Noble in one sitting. As I tossed down a shot, a thought occurred: what had happened to those sealed envelopes pressed into my mother's hands ... the bar mitzvah gifts ... expenses were involved, of course, in putting the feast together ... the hall rental ... and the rebbe himself had to be paid for instructing somebody teminally hopeless ... but ... I blessed myself ... blessed the schnaps ... and the woozies struck. The booze sent me into a spin. By moonlight I saw the clock reverse its hands. My bedroom floor, a whirlpool, was dragging me down. I jumped around like a carp out of water. I flopped in panic. Soon, the whirlpool dragged me under into a deep, merciful sleep, a greenish state, and then clouds shaped like kishka drifted as I swam in a private sky.

Deep Fried Dream

The ferocious dream I had, whereby the woozies released me to demons of the sub-galactic world:

I fall into a bog. The kishke clouds pass. I am staring at a silver screen illumed by a powerful prison lightbeam.
 "Can I get you something, kid?"
 The kid scrubs away a tear. The Father Confessor next to the kid bears resemblance to rebbe Noble.
 "Father, a nice onion pizza ..."
 "I can't do it kid. It's almost time."
 Father Love wants to tell the world they are all responsible for pulling the trigger, the kid didn't have a chance, born in the slums ... the school of hard-knocks ... his friends: pimps, prostitutes, perverts, drug addicts, cops on the pad. No, the kid didn't pull the trigger. It was hate, society, you and me, including Father Love. And now, they are playing God ... killing the kid ...
 Eddy, con #9 on Death Row, thoughtful as a tick drilling for blood, would dearly love to tear the collar from Father Love's neck.
 The film becomes grainy, crackles ... a cavity is present, a sepulchral silence.
 The only sound in the theatre: popcorn rattling in buttery containers, as usual before a death scene.
 The kid's upper lip quivers as though brushed by a religious firefly.
 The dream ruptures.
 "So why'd you do it, kid? All those nice goils ... aren't you ashamed, Eddy. Did you know your mother was a goil?"
 In the 40's, every celluloid degenerate's name was Eddy. Every prison priest had the flush of the bagman's worldly goodwill.
 The kid refuses to make eye contact. "Huh," he slobbers, guilt absent from his blue peepers. He is going to turn over those peepers to an eye bank ... maybe ... if Father Love can talk him into it.
 "Eddy, and you being from such a decent family ... you could have done the college ting like your brother, Eddy, you could have

amounted to somebody ... the president ... yes, Eddy, a fine ting ... democracy."

Eddy is boiling. Can he tell Father Love his mother was a whore ... a drugged wormy ...

"Back off ... screw ... you hear," he shouts.

"Eddy ... I'm not a copper ... Don't be mad, now. God will forgive you, in His Infinite Love ..."

"Don't call be Eddy ... only my pals call me Eddy ..."

"Okay, kid."

"I don't care about the Big Cheese up there. Maybe you'd like to meet that big Rat. Ha, ha, ha ..."

A hiss of air: "Help me, please ... I don't want to die." Father Love strokes the kid's hair. "Be brave ... I'll be with you ... so will He ..." The kid's face streaks with tears.

The kid starts giggling. He starts shivering and rubbing his hands together. He can feel the deeper chill entering his bones. He moans for his mother. The kid hates his mother.

"Please, please help me ..." It's time for one last confession. Not worth a nickle on Earth, maybe his soul has a little platinum. "Eddy ... let us pray."

The kid knows the game is up.

"You fruitbar ... I bet if I ripped that collar off your friggin neck."

"Eddy, don't mock ..." The kid's bawling like there's no tomorrow, which is accurate. There's the rhythm of rubber footsteps down the corridor, the cries of prisoners on Death Row. "I ain't afraid," says Eddy.

"Thou therefore, my son, be strong in the grace that is Jesus Christ ..."

The bulls move in and put the handcuffs on the kid. "It's okay, boys, I'm ready." They secure their special cuffs and chains, leading Eddy down the corridor, the confessor at his side. They stop before a steel door, the one with the red light above it. Eddy hands the confessor a crumpled piece of paper. "It's for mum ... I want her to have a few things ... it ain't much ..."

"I'll make sure she gets it. I promise."

The guards, ex-linemen for a college football team, drag the kid over the threshold. "Sometimes they foul themselves," says one of the bulls. "They do it all the time. But this kid's different."

"Goodbye kid ... see you in Heaven ..." Father Love shouts as the doors clang shut. They strap Eddy into his high chair. "I ain't scared," he says, screwing his lips tighter, peaceful as eggplant. He turns his eye to the porthole where the warden, his boys, a reporter (who harbors a special hate for degenerates like Eddy) and the confessor are peering into this strange spaceship.

"Show them how to die, Eddy ..." I shout into my pillow.

In the cramped theatre, kids are squirming on the plush, the girls sobbing for Eddy. "He looks kinda cute ..." The closest girl is probed by her boy friend, a blond chipper, trying to force his hand under her cotton dress, a punk with *wandering hand trouble*. "You're a wolf..." she cries. The rutting boy friend starts to wheeze like a young rodent in love ...

The bulls are placing a cheese-cloth over Eddy's face. One squeezes Eddy's shoulder. It's Porky's way of saying goodbye. Porky used to buy Eddy his *Old Gold* and warn the kid about the 'tubercules'. "We all got to shove off some time, Porky," Eddy used to say, offering the guard a weed.

Eddy's lips are moving.

The confessor strains for signals from under the deathveil: MUM ... is the Word.

A cyanide crystal ejected into a pail of sulphuric acid by remote control makes a sizzling sound, an Alkaseltzer tablet in a glass of cold water. A bell starts ringing ... a red light flares ...

A ghost fills the bowl of Eddy's skull. The confessor is making small animal noises.

Big Red, the tough-assed reporter who said dirty rats like Eddy deserved a sulphuric enema, turns away.

Eddy starts vibrating, convulsing slowly, then rapidly. His chest heaves, as if there were some huge rat in Eddy's chest. Eddy is straining to inhale the final vapours.

The young girl slaps her boy friend's hand just as he drives his tongue with animal joy into her ear ...

Eddy is dead. They all know it. The girls in the theatre ... their tumescent boy friends ... the confessor ... the warden ... Eddy's mother, still hooking on the street. Everybody knows Eddy is dead, except Eddy ...

The legs stop jerking against the steel bands, the rat in Eddy's chest is asleep, the fan on the wall is whirling, the confessor is crying. He knows Eddy's face has the color of broccoli, fresh, and in season.

The Meditation Tanks

Uncle Nathan reigned over a fish emporium on Baldwin Street, not far from the D'Arcy Street Talmud Torah. His dark fish tanks contained meditative creatures of sea and lake who stared vacuously at their closed perimeters before lapsing into a partial comatose state. The shop floor was inches deep in a carpet of sawdust to absorb gore, scales, and intestinal matter conglutinated with other intimate organs.

Every Friday, during the late forties and early fifties, a shade before sunset, I carried home packages of carp, pickerel, whitefish, and salmon-trout, selectively scaled, clipped and cut into generous portions by Nathan. Wrapped in layers of newspaper, the Neptunian confraternity appeared mummified. Fish blood, the ultimate glue, held the diversified corpus to the newspaper.

What disturbed me most was not the pieces of fish warming the mummifiing layers of newspaper but Nathan's gusto in the quick dismemberment. His gusto had deep suspicious undertones, even to a blooming teenager. His violence revealed a disturbed sublimated sexuality. The pieces of fish virtually exploded on his hard oak operating table, spurting little blood geysers, raising anatomical sectors ... an eye here, and there a white lung ... a pink heart ...

It seemed an endless wet dream, but what stabbed my curiosity was his manner of fondling them, arousing their libido ... somewhere in a vague erotic area of their infinitismal brains, a temporary pleasure principle was set in motion. Moments before their execution, they wheezed in a responsive anxiety while he sweated profusely.

The poor dwellers in those meditational tanks had the air of political prisoners, lipping out obscenities to their captor. Of course, depending on how religious or poetic one was, the odd torpedo carp or whitefish could just as easily have mouthed benediction. I like to think it was more a curse than prayerful utterance. No one has ever lip-read a fish before, but I learned to decipher the messages: an extreme distortion, a lip bending over another, meant the creature was venting hatreds, and therefore, his anger, or perhaps, her displeasure at Nathan, or anyone peering into the holding tank. Nathan paid little heed to these fine details. He kept cold water flowing into the tanks so the tribes remained vigorous until that eventual hour when he snuffed the batch of finned ethnicity, snuffed without the use of local anesthetic. A blow on the head was his method, and sometimes it required several vicious strokes with a club specially designated (called by contemporary anglers a 'priest' – but Nathan lived in the literal world: he never thought of calling his club a rabbi). His dispatcher's instrument was a small paddle. He rushed a wide butterfly net into the tank, scooping up a minor leviathan, dumping the beast on the terminal table, clubbing it into unconsciousness. I like to think the fish were dead when he clipped their fins, scrubbed their scales off their backs, and, wielding a miniature scimitar fish knife like Ming the Merciless, measured the meat for a few precious seconds, and then with the electric eye of a diamond cutter, split his tenants into even sections.

I assumed Nathan was courting a nervous breakdown, rebelling against ichtiocidal guilt by bashing that guilt out of existence. I recall the gasp of a creature not far from Death's fishing hole, a gasp microseconds before the animal was dismembered. Struck, the fish leaped off the surface of the sacrificial table but Nathan pounded it for good measure to ensure a swift demise, though sometimes he or she leapt again one last time. Another comrade followed, a fractured predecessor ... the knife and mallet readied in the restless tension of a Zen master ... the blade danced, another fish was stung ... fish after fish divorced from an alienated body ... it was all rhythm, sex, spontaneity ... a fish blood not nearly so red as our own, but more transparent, like ink in a cheap ballpoint pen ...

I developed an aversion to the fish blood from Nathan's emporium, and to this day I rub my hands together when the topic of blood comes up in lurid conversation, but as the blood gushed in every direction, Nathan darted a glance my way, and bashed his victim: it was all a process of the trade, sentimentality had no place in his establishment. The blow sent a shockwave through the shop, rattling the windows while the tub athletes flipped and were retired from active duty.

Nathan seemed inured to the slaughtering of his underwater legions. The question of launching his fish to the stars as an act of immorality never touched his heart and mind. A stronger point would have been: did he ever dine on his own fish? I never got around to asking him a few sensitive questions about the nature of the immutable and the noumenal, let alone fish and whether he felt that they had souls; and did mankind evolve from fish ... Nathan, tell me ... were you clubbing your prehistoric root ... ?

In truth, Nathan kept his feelings to himself and eked out his livelihood. He appeared to enjoy his work and his attitude to his fish possibly would not have been any different than Joe the Fruitman in Kensington market had you asked him in a moment when he was not busy serving his customers – what were his feelings about selling a large cabbage ... ?

The difference was that fish to Nathan were living edibles who had lips which he never tried reading. They were temporary guests in his ponds. Nathan suffered no fish-induced anxiety attacks ... oblong shadows semaphoring in the tanks had absolutely no impact on him ...

Nathan would have assumed that a goldfish was the freak of the batch which arrived in the iced fish crates and had, as a result of the extreme cold been slightly discoloured, or were they?

Of course, they had little time to develop any rapport: none of the tribe survived longer than a week. Friday was terminal city. There was no governor-reprieve. Nathan never succumbed to piscatorial liberalism. The complete hyberbole would have been Nathan closing the shop for a day and mourning their passing; the ultimate leap off-the-wall would have been Nathan opening a vegetable shop out of expiation (years later, after Nathan passed away, a mungbean health store opened on the same premises; the ghosts flip about after closing time ... fractions form into one solid fish ... they pout out their pain ...).

Nathan, depleting his fishy world, had a fish-like presence; while his heart wasn't grazed by guilt, his genes were. His psychic armour gave way at times to a deep brooding and a stillness came over him, like the quiescence of some channel fish. In Nathan's deep tubs thoughts bubbled up from the floor ... heavy thoughts ...

Like a carp, Nathan had wide thick shoulders, and he was short and stout; it was the compactness of a wide-bodied underwater animal ... and while often praising carp, he had a dyspeptic expression, as though everything in life tasted bitter, since there was more sweetness in heaven. The physical Earth was merely a sub station, one of many, in that long trek to parts unknown. In the meantime, we swam through life like bottom feeders – a carp or flounder, and found satisfactory edibles on the psychic floor, more readily available than bait fish above. Nathan stayed on the first level and was, as a result, constantly dour, one who believed you had to suffer on the bottom before reaching a school of bait fish residing in one's dreams.

Nathan's fish-like qualities reflected not only his sombre state (I don't ever recall him smiling on any of the Fridays I picked up my fish) but in the karmic outcome of his cruelty: his skin pores were broken and bleeding, similar to the large scales of the carp he had murdered. Fish scales stuck to his inflamed hands. Fish blood had dried and glued a grisly pattern onto those murderous fists so wide and thick, and to complicate his life and trade, he had one bum finger – white from his endless uncrating, unpacking, and sorting of fish from the ice crates. He had developed what is commonly known by carpenters and others who work in inclement weather as a 'dead finger'. It appeared oyster white, as did his face, which had only the slightest flush of health in his ruddy cheeks. When he worked fast and furiously, a fog emanated from the crates, enshrouding him ... a spectre from the aquatic cosmos attacking his bones ...

It was his cold selection finger. Nathan plucked those chub, or whitefish that were still breathing through the ice slivers, and dropped them into the holding tanks where they gradually came out of their deep sleep. The other deep sleepers were displayed in the shop window. They were gruesome against the background of ice chips, exhibited in an open casket ... a ghoulish sense of humor on Nathan's part ... It was the embalmer in his personality. In truth, Nathan enjoyed his work, and if he indulged in rude display of his fishly wares, then he could be forgiven his indulgences. Every trade has an occupational hazard. He measured his fish with a deep sense of pride. He lived through his fish in the same way parents live through their children. The man never sold a bad fish to anyone and this was evident on Friday when his shop was crammed with customers. They expected the best and received the best of freshest fish, gutted, scaled ... A customer pointed to a carp and Nathan lowered his net ... his mood *concealed*. In his substance, a form of mysanthropy dwelt: the mysanthrope swam like a sardine shark attacking some unsuspecting tourist in the tropics – the devil or devils enter the bowels of their victims, ripping them to pieces ... A psychic sardine-shock seemed to follow Nathan around in his shop as he mumbled incoherent words, totally alienated, until a shiny fish appeared ... and his detached grimace became something close to being a smile.

Nathan needed diversion. His energies needed to be channelled elsewhere, into something more creative. I'd have preferred him as a collector of bad debts, a phantom with the atomic particles of Al Capone, Scarface, Edward G. Robinson, the bon-bon particles of Nathan, all adding up to Big Eddy and efficiency. Eddy runs an outfit called the Piranha Acceptance Corporation, or PAC, as it is known on the street. A defaulter has disregarded Big Eddy's final notice. The greaseball, a pimply-faced hustler who dominates a few hard street corners, won't pay interest on his loan, won't pay his fifty bills a week, and this has caused gas bubbles in Big Eddy's stomach. The punk has let it be known that the warning is worth less than asswipe: this has given Big Eddy heartburn. The only ant-acid is maybe chop a finger off, for good measure ...

The dirty little punk is picked up by Big Eddy's gorillas, a standard bunch in their two-tone pointed shoes and creamy white suits ... black shirts and white ties ... hair is pressed flat with Wildroot Cream Oil ... and they carry the skinny meatloaf along the street to a cream-coloured convertible. They drive away with their delinquent account, who is sweating in the back seat. He knows it is wise to say nothing. They would love to damage his body before handing it over to Big Eddy. The machine stops at an ugly semi-detached house. They are greeted by two nasty doberman. The phantom blows a whistle, the two monsters disappear. The punk is again lifted by his elbows; fright sets in like rigor mortis. They carry him into Big Eddy's den with its phony fireplace. Big Eddy is staring into an aquarium. A rumbling noise issues from the tank, a thick-faced fish staring through the glass, the black torpedo opens his jaws – revealing a set of upper and lower needle works.

Eddy feels affection for his pet. He has fed it fingers, chicken, goldfish, and various strains of cat food ... concerned that his charge is missing a mixed diet ... too overweight ... arterial sclerosis, a heart attack ... he ... she ... certainly no eunuch ... as Big Eddy strokes his gold-edged razor, everyone is all ears, including the punk.

Then, a little appetizer before the morality play. Eddy is scraping hair off his hands, a ritual he's been through before. He plucks a hair from the back of his head, slices it as though it were greased in butter. Dorthy, his pet piranha, has not had her mid-day meal. She is Dorthy, though Eddy's never really determined the gender of his aquatic pal. Dorthy, in honor of his first wife, who wore Lamour-like sweaters and was also picked up at a drugstore counter, spinning on her stool.

"Schmuck, you missed a payment," says Eddy. The punk shrugs. "Screw you," he says. Eddy is in a meaner mood than Dorthy, the lunatical eating machine. The shine on those teeth ... the minty breath ... Dorthy of the clean gleamers, capped ... a dental surgeon's wet dream ...

There's an electrical glee in the fish.

"What did you say, punk?"

"You heard me," snaps the meathead, sneering into Eddy's face.

"I must be hearing things," Eddy says with a Dorthy-like leer. The boys nod like true robotons. Eddy grips the punk's wrist and gives him a burn. Those are worker's hands. Eddy used to butcher pork in a slaughterhouse.

"You heard me, SLIME BALL," the punk says, playing the Big Bluff.

Eddy gives the punk a third-degree burn on the wrist. "Okay boys, let's make some pastrami out of this sucker ..." The punk feels warm piss trickling down his pant leg.

"Hey, wormface," Eddy screams, "you aint never gonna use your pinkies on your broad again. Nobody shits on me and walks away ... nobody."

"Please ... Eddy ..." The punk's voice-box is working but the voice doesn't belong to him.

"I'm gonna clip your little wee finger and feed it to Dorthy cause she loves them fingers." Big Eddy breaks out into a gust of laughter. Everybody's laughing but the punk. Dorthy is laughing in her tank. She has a tight pepsodent smile.

The torpedos hold the punk down. "I'm just gonna chop that little finger, the one with the phony ice ..."

"Eddy, I can explain ... no ..."

The punk sees his pinkie and ring gobbled by Dorthy. He goes into a spin, passing out on the rug, his stump spurting red juice. Eddy has a red-hot curling iron to staunch the bleeding. Eddy fancies himself a finger specialist.

Dorthy chews, burps.

"You know boys, I love the sound she makes. That's real music, not the canned shit ..."

The punk comes to, smells the singe of burning flesh, and passes out again. Eddy shoves an ammonia vial under the punk's nose.

"Oh ...oh ... God ... oh MOM ..."

"Hey wormbag ... You must have chocolate ladyfingers. Dorthy likes you... And it aint Mom ... MUM's the WORD."

There was a sleek little Dorthy in every customer crowding into Nathan's claustrophobic shop. There was a lot of piranha in Nathan, too. He knew how to deal with boistrous housewives maligning or molesting his fish. "That fish was stale ... such fish you should throw in the garbage ... to fool an old lady?"

Nathan endured the Friday Harpies. It was bad enough when they fondled his fish, but suggesting his fish were not fresh when he himself kept them under cold showers, and for no longer than a week in their tub, pressed on his heart. Jabbing a deadly finger, he dimmed their invective, continued his butchery, his place of extermination, sometimes flinging a fish head down on the table, splashing the women with blood. That had a cooling effect. The newspapers stacked to the ceiling were rapidly depleted. He pulled on a white cone of string suspended from the ceiling, yanking an arm's length of cord, sweeping loops around each bundle, securing a favorite knot. A bundle of fish was shoved into his customer's hands, a flush of anger in his cheeks, but no sound came from his lips; his eyes were fixed on their's and it was not a friendly entrepreneurial gaze, but a predacious force whose negative vibrations rattled the shop windows. Nathan, rather than endure an argument with a customer, generously added an extra fish body. Each paid and made for the door passing the antique cash register that he rarely if ever used. Nathan liked something more personal, an old cash drawer at the back of the shop. After his apron pockets were loaded with bills and coins, he pulled the drawer out and stuffed the money in, and if there was a free moment, he would clean the coins and bills, wipe off the fish blood, guts, and scales, handling the bills which he rolled into a tube and tied down with an elastic. He carefully stacked his coins: nickles, dimes, fifty cent pieces, silver dollars; not a square inch of space was wasted. His accounting system was sufficient. It didn't impede his progress.

Nathan's sink was broken down. He stopped to scrub blood off his face, and wiped his hands on a soiled towel. A shard of mirror hung from a nail. He stared into the mirror, flicked away some scales, brushed his hair away and turned back to his chores. He had, along with his other implements, a special triton to keep the dead and dying at bay. Sometimes a fish head sought its severed body, a tail favoured a particular anatomical part, flipping toward union. Nathan brought his triton into play, pronging the piece to the surface of the table. It was ancient, it was magic.

He could have waved it at his cantankerous customers but his stare was enough... an insult mumbled and regurgitated... He regurgitated anger and it sublimated itself in his actions as he flung a huge cod head onto the antique scale, shifting the weights until the balance steadied in an even horizon while Nathan fried his customers with his eyes. The frame of the scales was cast iron and parts were bronze. He patiently waited for the correct weight and never rushed, although his fingers fluttered while the machinery was in motion.

Nathan always kept me off balance, in motion for a fist full of silver and, when he was in a more generous mood, a five spot. I had to clean the shop, sweep the floor and shovel contaminated sawdust into a bin along with offal and an assortment of guts. There had to be a fresh carpet of sawdust and the tanks had to be scrubbed and cleaned. Nathan had a steel scrub brush. He expected spotless scrubbing and sweat and rhythm, for no matter how much energy I put into the scrubbing, it was never quite enough. It was always blood he imagined he saw.

The sour-smelling sawdust and pails of offal were loaded along with broken fishcrates onto an old railway wagon which Nathan pulled out of the alleyway next to his shop. Together, we piled fish crates and forced the pails in, pressing them into the wood, crushing the containers. I hauled the rusted creaking wagon down the road, turning the corner at Henry Street and at last going along a laneway at the back of the shop. I had to be careful pulling the load, piled so precariously, but somehow I managed to get the wagon down the lane, stopping at Nathan's yard. I tossed the crates over a high fence. Bits and pieces of offal mixed in sawdust fell back on me. A fishhead would fly at my face ... some lung ... guts ... I reeked of decaying fish. I kicked at the cats meowing around my legs. I stood on a crate and peered into Nathan's yard, discovering sunflowers bending their heads, the tallest sunflowers in the neighborhood ...

I dragged the wagon back to the shop where Nathan was still hosing down the tanks. A bundle of fish was on the table and an envelope of bills. Nathan was extremely generous this day. I didn't ask any questions. I thanked him for the fish and the money. He rarely replied. I was fortunate to be blessed with a grump and nothing more. I faithfully carried the palpitating bundle home, stripped the paper, dumped the fish into a sink of cold water, and the pieces took on a life of their own ... a fish head lipped an obituary ...

Under a lightbulb casting a sallow yellow light, Nathan moved in shadows, Nathan ready with his net, Nathan staring into the holding tank ... as the bubbling increases in the water, the carp smacking the water with its tail, staring wall-eyed at life. There is a form of thought transference taking place between Nathan and his fish. I view the fish as being a diminuition of Eddy. They are all waiting for the red lightbulb to flare. Their appeal has been turned down.

Birth of a Liberal: 1947, 1948

A few teachers at Lansdowne Public school loomed larger than a summer flounder. They were veterans fresh from the battlefields of Europe, or British transplants who found themselves in a holding tank, or poor fish who dreamt of English barons pulling King John's elbows at Runnymede, June 15, 1215, extracting liberties ... politics as dentistry.

They suffered from Anglophilia, revering all things British. They believed in their long bones that Britain was the cradle of civilization. If you'd said that the Chinese invented paper and discovered gun powder just when the tribes of Britain, painted a nice blue, were introduced to Roman lead plumbing, they'd have put your name in a dark book, a possible Bolshie ... in the Red bud ...

Mr. Chick, an endearing character who had the oily efficiency of a British drill sergeant, was my grade seven history teacher. He had a magnificent obsession, the Battle of Hastings. He chalked out the whole psychic relief-map of the war between the Saxon defenders and Norman invaders on a blackboard under a massive headline: HASTINGS, 1066.

Mr. Chick was almost seven feet tall, or so it seemed to us munchkins, as he let his long arms wag while he chalked spasmodic X's or a swooping footnote. Needless to say, his heart was with the Saxons, but it was a wonderful bias; the man tried to be *frightfully* objective as a *historian*. Normans, those dastardly foreigners, had invaded Britain, landing on pure Anglo-Saxon soil, intending to make slaves of the peasant folk, get in a little bit of looting ... (Chick never dared mention rape –) and were met by King Harold and his lads 'good and bold', battle-armed to the pearly white teeth (Chick's dentition shone as he waxed on about wonderful Harold ... tall in the saddle ... his men emboldened by example ...) and as a fair footnote to the Norman chieftain, Chick mentioned a tiny episode: the warlord had fallen off his horse, but being quick-witted and no slouch, scooped up a handful of sand: "Comrades, I've scarce arrived and already Britain is mine and yours." The sand trickled from his palm, his men cheered, and a bad fall had been converted into symbolic victory, a divine revelation (Oh, Eddy, Eddy, where was the handful of sand when you needed it?).

From the start, God was leaning over Harold's shoulder, bleaching his blonde hair with Eternal Light; a vulturous shadow hovered over the invaders. This was no ordinary battle, but one between the forces of light and darkness. We were naturally with the forces of light, and to root for the Normans would have meant an after-hours detention for life. We were as quiet as carp.

Chick was doing a dance, his lanky body swaying to the rhythms of mortal battle, to death, to cowards in the rear, come on boys ... fight fight fight ... let them feel your blades ... hip ...hip for Harold ...hooray ... Chick never explored the theological ramifications of the battle's outcome. It was his blind spot, a source of anguish, and globules of sweat fell from Chick's forehead, vintage 1066 ... The room temperature went up, Chick reached his climax ... his blue eyes about to pop, caught like a mayfly on the riffles of a historic current and trouts of happiness were nipping at his wings. History sucked him into a whirlpool, he swayed in the grips of high emotion as he curiously cross-hatched the gory moments and then, ZAPPO ... wham-bang ...brave King Harold got stung full in the eyeball by a lucky and treacherous Norman arrow.

Chick stopped to emphasize the gaping vicious wound, the slender sleek arrow, grunting, and even moaning softly. We were terrified. I realized what this meant and how utterly demoralizing for England: the forces of light, and Harold's fighting comrades ... I pulled the arrow out of *my* eye socket ... a ruptured oyster... with fibre ... bloody ... the pain intense ... lodged so deeply ...

Chick wheezed, his thin body swaying to some sun god ... Chick going through the agony of defeat: "Brave Saxons, throw down your weapons ... you have fought a good battle ..." Chick hauled at his eyeball, dragging that mental arrowhead out ... He took his time, twisting, pulling, and it was a lean arrow ... longer than usual ... it was his special exorcism ... and we dignified his psychic disturbance by listening and not making rude noises. Chick was dying for Harold. Harold and Chick were one. Harold died on the field for Chick ... the eyeball bursting ... I know that pain: once, while fishing at summer camp, I hooked a sunfish in the eye. The animal twisted on the hook. Chick twisted in his dance. Harold had twisted in his pain. My sunfish died in '47, Chick got his in 1066.

Chick's cross-hatchings filled the blackboard, arrows engulfed the sky. It was Chick's way of saying it would have been easier for a camel to enter through the eye of a needle than for some poor duck to fly through his sky of factotum. We never had a chance in that slivered atmosphere, the air was pregnant with arrowheads, just like the day Harold got his. The whole blackboard was an Eric Satie score to the gods ... Seismographically speaking, we were held by descriptions of carnage, thousands of corpses cross-hatched on the battlefield, Harold roaring in pain ... my eye ... God ... my eye. Chick was breathless, white as his catharsis. I meant to ask him how many horses had died that day ... But it would have been in vain. Being a captive audience, we had absorbed his shame and shock of defeat. In his defeat lay his dignity. Therein lies pure poetry, a powerful purgative in Chick's repressed landscape. Twenty years later, he and others would have worked it out through primal therapy. Chick sagged for a moment, spent, then straightened up, brushed back his hair, tucked his tartan tie into his suit coat and flashed a feeble smile.

"Never, *never* give up ... you are made of sterner stuff, lads," Chick said. Suddenly he broke into a wide, almost supernatural, smile, supernatural because it had little or no relationship to the rest of his face. A detached grin, extraneous, but a smile with its own integrity, a smile to diminish mortal smiles ... "Never ... never ..." King Chick boomed. He puffed his chest out. "One battle lost does not a war lose ... Remember that, lads, when your time for lost battles comes."

"Yes Sir," roared the class. Chick marched the length of the blackboard, as though doing penance, moving back and forth, turning to shake his head in disbelief ... Oh Hastings, Hastings.

Chick's teeth seemed to be snowing. He had a hopeful smile. I had come to recognize phases of his smile, secrets in nuance ... humble, arrogant, playful, angry, all tributaries of a central smile. You kept your distance when the smile waned ... when he was in a state of thought-transference, sitting silently at his desk facing his class, his spine straight as a British bayonet. Chick discovered I had a budding curvature of the spine: and something had to be done about my disorder, my spine somehow straightened. I was told to press a blackboard-pointer to the small of my back and stand firmly at attention, chin up, eyes front. I stood at the back of the class and Chick kept his lights on me. "Chest out, lad," he roared, a friendly roar followed by an epiglotal laugh, trailed by a smile of encouragement. There was no damned way Chick was going to tolerate a hunchback in his group. Chick meant well and, alas, saw the shape of things to come.

"Godsakes, straighten up, lad..." He marched by showing me how to straighten my shoulders. "Throw those shoulders back, eyes front, chin up ..." "Yes Sir," I snapped, straightening the pointer until it almost sang.

Chick had several other ants in his spiritual craw. For example, at the snap of his fingerbone, we jumped like tiny jacks out of some emotional box, dashing twice around our desks and down we'd blast into our seats when he snapped his fingerbone for the second time. I watched this disciplinary drill from the back of the room where I was doing my spinal exercises ... But no one resented Chick's drills. The man's eccentricities were a welcome relief. He was fair. Chick displayed no malice toward any child who failed his marching orders. There was only his displeasure smile, a slight droop of the lip, but no droop in his spirit, because he also had a fine brimstone fever. Muscle-tone of the mind. He made us memorize Isaiah. First thing in the morning, someone would recite a particular passage ... the student delivering a line from memory and the class coming up with the following line ... *And they shall beat their swords into plowshares*, and they sang *And their spears into pruninghooks.*

If a student faltered, and the silence became unbearable, Chick then boomed out the line. The students bellowed back. It was all angelic music to his ears. Chick was an ecstatic, his eyes shining like freshly minted dollars

Nation shall not lift up sword against nation

Chick beamed in the Creator's holy radium and raised his sonorous voice, his face calm, the flesh bright with rejuvenation, his blue eyes bluer

Neither shall they learn war anymore

How did these pacifist lines gell with glorification of the gore at Hastings? Chick had a fissure in his logic. Like many a man in his tweedy mind, he gloated over violence provided he took no part in any hairy war. The man was both mental warrior and lover of Biblic lambs, the contradictions of hope wherein

... the wolf shall dwell with the lamb,
And the leopard shall lie down
with the kid;
And the calf and the young lion
and the fatling together;
And a little child shall lead them.

There was a child in Chick, a little lamb, and some ham as well whenever he heard the Lord calling from over a high mountain

And the lion shall eat straw like the ox
And the sucking child shall play
on the hole of the asp,
And the weaned child shall put
his hand on the basilisk's den.

Gratitude rumbled up from his stomach, issuing from his pearly mouth. I had chanted Isaiah in the *Tenach* in ancient Hebrew, a language I didn't understand, written down in soiled Hebrew prayer books, but it was Chick, that eccentric Christian who led me to the illuminative poetry of the major Hebrew prophet, opening a place in my brain pan for the power of language and the meaning of poetics ... implanting the first sprouts on the bald pate of my muse ...

He was, you see, a liberal, and that took a certain amount of courage in a world of pain ... courage and cosmetics. He reeked of cologne while sweating profusely, furiously mopping his brow with a perfectly pressed handkerchief. Is this the fate of the liberal? Nervous twitching, a stiff-legged walk, an iron rod pinned through the spinal column, always on the verge of ecstacy or tears. Dead, perhaps the living dead ... never guilty of bad posture, and he really did wash behind his ears, so that they shone like his teeth, and his Lone Ranger smile matched his starched gray flannel trousers, and the light bounced off his leather elbow-patches that matched his brogues, and his broad-cloth shirt was laundered to death so that it sang in all its whiteness, shining like a slug in sunlight, and only the fearful tartan tie broke the symmetry.

Neatness. Did it grow on his person like a fungus. Neatness. Life as a folded letter.

I was sure he boiled his spoons, wore white gloves in the evening to ward off *spiritis herpes facialis* ... fatal kiss of a luna moth ... and sure he was addicted to green soap ... as the flypaper of dementia unrolled its long tongue and followed the man everywhere ... shadowing him like a sad mist where tubercules sang out to him in the evening ... ah, he was a liberal; he lived through wish fulfilment, an arrow in his soul, but in an era of schoolboy corporal punishment – which worked its way through the body politic with the ferocity of a maggot plunging into meat – Chick was a liberal luxuriating in the romance of gore, reluctant to harm the terrorizing fly, let alone a child. There was no strapping in his cloakroom ... It was all logic ... and pristine presentation ... drills, drills, cologne and a military liberalism ... the voice of authority proved potent, a pointer pressed against the curved spine. The voice of the Empire, scrubbed behind the ears.

"A Chinaman Can Do It"

Anyone passing Crunchdale pissed their pants. Crunchdale, his face cratered by chicken pox, caught a nervous tick denoting mischief, grabbed a kid, tweaking his cheek into an involuntary smile on the spot. Tears meant his *medicine* was working, inducing fear, which translated into *respect*. Magically, Chick materialized after a tweaking, like a mortician warming up to a stiff, extending a pressed clean white handkerchief to a boy who had saved his tears, bursting into a sobbing gush as the monogrammed cloth passed before his eyes (the good cop, the third degree and the degree of grace ... Broderick Crawford, where were you then, where are you now?).

"Now, sonny ... here you are ..."

Sometimes for civility's sake, Chick and Crunchdale appeared in the halls chatting amiably, co-existing, respecting zones of influence. They kept their distance, two plague ships passing in the night: you stopped dead in your path when Chick clanged the school bell, and with a second ringing, you marched to the entrance and lined up quietly. Chick the dipstick cop, Crunchdale the hardnosed meatball...

Chick was invisible whenever Crunchdale grabbed a student by the scruff of his neck, seized the shortest hair on the hairline, and began twisting that shoot ... twisting ... until his victim went into hysterics, howling, delicious music to Crunchdale. A pygmy dervish spun around ... and Chick was always nowhere when Crunchdale performed his hairy symphony: how many orthodontists ... lawyers ... nose-bobbers and nabobs ... real estate barons and buffoons had a twist, did a dance, and were shaped by Crunchdale's fingers, fear working like a sardine-shark nipping the bowels ... the boy mewing like a wounded lamb ... Crunchdale capped his hair-twisting with a backhander, a skilful blow that didn't draw blood, a rosy protrusion ... but no blood ... Crunchdale was particularly careful about ears. No ruptured eardrums, and no blow to the eyes ... nose ... mouth. He had a delicate sense of those who might make him twist in the wind, parents turned blood-thirsty by blood of their blood. He was a cheek man and expert in hairlines. And then a handkerchief appeared, Chick smiling the way Jesus smiled in all the Salvation Army posters ... Let Rome have its due ... taxes ... as the flesh was rendered unto Crunchdale ... Thus the cuffed boy gathered his marbles, his head singing like a canary ... it was hard to hold onto the balance wheel ... the blow had disconnected the cerebral wiring ... Some boys, stunned, made a slight woofing sound ...

Crunchdale loved dogs.

And then there was Miss Plover, who put her whole being into a good strapping. She had one arm; the other had been amputated at the elbow. Her one good hand was for holding up the bible or laying on the leather. She explored a student's hand, read his palm for pain points. She stood back. The strap sailed, cutting the meat at the wrist-bone, and then another and another, her breath up and down like an asthmatic vole in heat. She pounded our meat. After a session with Stumpy Plover we washed our hands in cold water to keep down the bruises ... the throbbings ... the burn ... Bleeders were sent directly to the nurse's office. Hush. Hush. Ice in the office. But at least Miss Plover didn't tap you across the cheek for good measure. I still remember her swaying, some flautist playing *Aves* inside her skull, holding the bible up with her good hand, emphasizing her point by wagging the stump ...

Sometimes Crunchdale cocked his head and stared scornfully at the one-winged warrior. Crunchy had the munchies for girls in transition between dolls and lipstick. He was a tit-feeler, and explored more than a few acorns, and so set his beams not on the Plover but on Gloria. A tropical flush seeped into the cratered flesh of his face. Oh, he never strapped a girl. He was a coddler, a cuddler. He loved dogs and little girls with budding acorns. Beaming at his child brides, his Gloria – who suddenly understood the power a flower has in opening to the sun.

"You can do it ... For God's sake ... a Chinaman can do it ..."

His hand was on Gloria's shoulder, then her neck, under the curled brown hair, massaging. "You can do it for God's sake ..."

Gloria smiled. The room sat still, suspended in Crunchy's tropical humidity.

"Add up that column ..."

I tried concentrating: should I carry the number over to another column.

"It's easy ... a Chinaman can do it," he growled.

Crunchy, I failed and you cuffed me, and I have carried your memory over to the next column.

Manny

Every school has its lunatic: a child from a broken home, a budding psychopath lopsided in the brainpan. A time bomb, Manny had to be disconnected. He had a nasty habit, carrying razor blades into the classroom. The rub was, no bug house in the land would store a junior lunatic unless he had *offed* his folks and gotten printer's ink in the way of news. There was talk about hauling him away to a special trade school (possibly the very institution some teacher had in mind for me), but that was only rumor and the loose lip. So, Manny – whose lip sometimes hung a little loose – kept on bringing razors to class, with a growth of peach fuzz on his face and a wild leer in his brown eyes. He smelled of urine and once in a while the teacher quietly opened a window when the whole room took on the tang of a washroom. Everybody kept their distance. They realized that the slightest remark could transform him into a demon ... frothing like a deranged animal and peeing in protest. Even Crunchdale avoided him; while he liked dogs, he was nervous about a demented boy whose unwholesome habit was biting – as his was hair-tugging. Manny's teeth were rotten, his mouth stank, and a bite was dangerous. A few boys regarded Manny as their secret weapon, their defense against pain, tagging behind him when they passed Crunchdale who pretended during class that the sighs, whimpers and sobbings came not from Manny but from steam pipes along the walls and ceiling. And an almost indistinct hissing noise ... pee running along the aisle ... was a portent of inner lunatic pain, and Crunch was no fool ... he left the leakage there. It was a lesson learned from a man who loved dogs: always be prepared to leave a little leakage. I wonder if Manny ever received a report card, and if he did, who did he show it to?

Magic Voyeurism

I heard the steady hum of printing presses on Sussex street. Like wolves who had come into their oestrus cycle, we moved over the bins where tons of Sunbathing magazines had been discarded. We reached out for the solarography, pulling armfuls of printed pages still warm from the presses. They were discolored, oily, some pages bound, others partially collated. We were minnows in life's filthy stream of smiling couples in the buff, their smiling brood in birthday suits.

I had no interest in the family unit ... they were less appealing than any carp with its immense scales swimming in one of Nathan's fishtanks ... carp so naturally filled out with a healthy lustre to their appearance ... and besides, whoever thought of carp being too thin, obese ... underdeveloped ... skin problems? The young twiggy women were succulent as speckled rainbow trout in season. A tall women with small breasts was the stuff of dreams priapismatic ... those glossy photos were as steamy as a Kensington Market bakery on Sunday morning. It took years to comprehend the implications of such haute voyeurism.

In a sense, the glossies were better than getting laid years down the road; they left something for the wicked imagination to probe, while the real McCoy dispelled every wild illusion. The feral creatures in the woods of my mind were laughing at me. You sucker, sneered the groundhog – pictures are worth more than a thousand words because everything eventually is stripped to the bone and the final result of stripping is the deep and easy sleep ... excitement is in the illusions we groundhogs lost with the first winter. Only the shadow really knows.

I hogged the magazines; they were my mental funhouse and very affordable. There the soul was trapped in the photograph and the nudist had given away his soul to the *public*. The savage in me thought the unprotected image of the self too vulnerable. What did nudists sell their soul for? Were they some Evangelical cult for nudity? Did they do it for love? And now were their souls in cold storage forevermore? Nudists for God? And why in blazes were they always smiling as if they'd just been drugged?

Nobody was going to steal my soul because I wasn't going to join this zany crowd down at Buff Beach. I enjoyed cutting open the multiple pages, finding the ideal sex symbol, a young tanned woman straight as a teen-aged willow with a modest Venus mound ... I could have steamed open those pages with my bated breath. I assumed decent folk were born into clothes as some animals naturally evolve into a glossy pelt. Benny had once confided to me that clothes were meant for humans in the same way a set of fairy wings belonged to a house fly. We were meant for clothes not because of torturous elements: ice ... snow ... rain ... frogs ... fish falling from the sky ... but because the flesh itself, in extreme modesty, craved clothes as dry bones need an adhesive agent to glue down the skin. Does a duck sunbathe nude? Wasn't Hoppy tall in the saddle in his sharp clothes? Only his horse was nude ... Carp, at least, have scales ... trout, a mucous membrane to protect its body ... They are natural flashers ... inoffensive ... fitting into the natural order ... melding into the ecological chain ... Nudists, crave *psychic clothes*, a sun tan ... a dermal layer of clothes ... they are clearly exhibitionists who have gone over the flasher's horizon ... they've long ago discarded their trenchcoats ...

Fish have the decency to *hide* from public view.

The white folk flexed their muscles ... *bronzed* biceps ... they were body-builders for the glory of God ... muscles and a deep sun tan ... but there was more ... the porphyroid flawless people became the bronzed family unit sucking-up to the sun as a bee to the sunny powder of a hollyhock ... health food ... essential golden pollen ... secret bread ... so what was the obsession with a bronzed body? The common denominator in those magazines, it seemed, was a fixation – the bronzed beautiful. A few abnormal sun fanciers were flung in among the pages: dwarves ... midgets ... the token hunchback ... an obese man or woman ... and even an androgyne ... a vague attempt to tone down the Apollo complex ... but in the raw ... the force of the meat was with the very well hung male, tall and blonde ... and his counterpart in the opposite gender: the wide hipped and abundantly bosomed woman, also blonde ...

There were a few narrow-hipped females, whippets in the *minority*, nymphets running around the beach ... close to the family unit, all linked in a ring of smiles ... fixed ... not only their personalities but their jaws had been anaesthetized for all eternity ... bronzed as some bronze their baby shoes ...

But there was a dark malevolent undercurrent in these solar-loving magazines: food for every brain: the gay-bi male and female could ogle the image of their choice ... and there was ammunition for the paedophile ... naked pubescence in the nuclear family ... And supposing you were a tri-sexual cannibal; then your eyes would run in glad glue...

The photographic detail was impeccably clear and intimate from a safe distance: you did not have to *sweat* among these sun-lovers ... Nobody would laugh at your physical imperfections ... you could stare contemptuously as they made fools of themselves ... the mind has an intensity equal to the pulsing parts of the sexual economy – and it could be aroused to heights greater than the carnal. The brain with its billions of freeways and concession roads to an eroto-chemistry: that gray protoplasm is both projectionist and projector of stimulating images long after other portions of the body have completed their act; thoughts secreting themselves into the pores of the memory sponge...

They glare at me still from those high-gloss pages ... they surface away from spouse and brood ... glaring at me with unblemished faces ... the blonde Aryanized woman with wide hips and large breasts ... her smile muscle-bound ... and the husband, his huge snake an entity in itself, hanging like a thick vine ... and the same smile ... detached...

As for the boys at the print shop, the presses hummed but did their heads sing? The same question can be begged from a baker: do the enzymes scream when dough rises in the pans of heated ovens? Does wheat germ have feeling? Does yeast break down...?

Perhaps the printer was a hunchback who resented all stiff-spined folk, all straight-haired freaks ... grinding away at his job, he has nothing against the solar system. He worships the moon. The phallus head of the Creator may impregnate the world, while our planet cooks in that sex ... crocuses bloom ... cabbages laugh under their many leaves ... and the *mother naked* crowd goes on tanning ... but the printer, he was alone, unmoved in his inky light.

Who among them, printer and nudists, cared about the Battle of Hastings? The only meaningful arrow in their skinscape was an erection faster than any speeding arrow splitting King Harold's lightbeam. This was the real stuff. They blew out Harold's eyeball because they meant business. War is the best jerkoff of all. All those generals beating their steel meat, the deeper penetration of death. My mottled obsession with the unblemished, my voyeurism was healthier by far than any Norman arrow singing into a brain...

Scott

Colonel Scott, he of grade eight literature, was a Tory, from thin pencil-moustache to pointed black shoes. He lectured us on the glories of the Empire, unrolling a global map from above the blackboard, laying his pointer upon the British Reich thickly blobbed in scarlet. His moustache flickered like a snail, and his gray eyes flared when he came to Bolshevism, the other empire, evil, Godless...

Scott fulminated. His face paled, the blood ceasing to course, leaving him pallid while he pounded the pointer for freedom, family, church, God and democracy – but not necessarily in that order.

There was another chart in the classroom and it stood next to the cloakroom. Its bucolical tones glued our attention: it had the appearance of a health chart, a balanced diet ... but that was a device, for this was a chart of a different stripe. Several cows stared out at the viewer: there were *cows* representing capitalism and freedom; there were fewer cows representing socialism; but the lone Bolshevik cow was the most pathetic of all ... lonely, thin, emaciated so that its rib cage protruded. This was the price of Communism; the state grabbed your cows ... your livestock was nationalized; the state took your individuality ... The red British Empire was protective, civilizing, but the dark empire ... the Red octopus was cruel ... barbaric ... Democracy, God, family ... and who among us would have challenged Britain's barbarism in India, Africa? Scott glittered like a banker, everything about the man starched. He, too, suffered from intense hygiene. He had a pin-stripe contempt for the apathy of the unwashed and unknowing.

He smacked his pointer across his knee, instilling a love of Kipling in us, a love of patriotic poetry. The rhyming line and the thin Red line. A line of blood between barbarism and a jolly good show. I was all for the show, at the Alhambra or Midtown. One afternoon I went to the movies, to Four Feathers, a Korda production about a man who refused to join his comrades by volunteering to join General Gordon in the Sudan. He was deemed a coward and sent a white feather, a symbol of cowardice. To make up for that taunt, he took a more circuitous route so he could link up with his comrades who were under dire attack. I gasped as waves of Arabs and Pygmies undulated across the desert and charged the Red Square. Breathless, I told Scott about the film. He listened politely. "They broke the Square, sir," I said.

"Who did?" Scott asked cooly.

Gasping for the words, I blurted out, "Why sir, the FUZZY WUZZIES" (I had it directly from a sergeant in the flick as he fell to the ground, a Pygmy's spear upright in his gut: "Fuzzy ... ugggh ... Wuzzies ...").

Stony silence: Scott's blonde hair was the sergeant's on the sand ... blood seeping ...

"Yes," Scott replied. "That's exactly how it happened." He smiled sadly and chewed a little lozenge to freshen his breath.

The Vampire

After the school day dissolved, we retired to the schoolyard where the action was marbles and fast silver. A kid steadied a fifty-cent-piece against a marble and then stood well back from that mottled planet. Directly facing him, another boy directed a beam of concentration on the target which was worth half a week's allowance, a tidy fortune for a twelve year-old, and an absolute disaster to lose. The boy behind the coin made immediate eye contact with the kid about to propel a bullet of a marble at the silver face. He was some thirty to forty feet away, behind a chalked line, concentrating his psychic stare, and the more his cerebral energy, the closer the coin and marble eyeball appeared. The banker kept eye contact, hoping to throw his opponent off by sheer will power. It was a test of faith: one wave of electro magnetic force meeting another, bending it like a spoon, slightly...

Kneeling behind the chalked line, the shooter hoped to be the executioner with his magic marble: the cosmic blast, the trigger-finger exercised, the knuckle snapped, and then the legal reach of the marksman's hand across the line. The entrepreneur of the shooting lane realized the odds were in his favor, but the possibility was there of losing his money, if not in the first shot, then the second: the shooter had purchased several marbles at approximately half the value of the coin he was going to send into an orbicular spin (they were larger marbles than those on the shooting lanes, fatter)... and more veins seemed to reside under the surface of the marble: the odds were sixty percent for the house and forty for the player, and the odds increased substantially for the nervous little fellow facing the shooter. There were more nerves alive in the shooting lanes than in the ganglion in the marble...

A glob of spit slid from a lower lip and fell to the pavement where it lay, a transparent glue. This marksman was not just any shooter, he was taking on the airs of a blood eater...

He cracked his knuckles, stretched his finger taut, twinked his eye muscles, rotated his neck, and to everybody's amazement – and the entrepreneur's grief – a winning light surrounded him, a play of light in late March, glancing off the small shoulders of the vampire. Other boys, and a few girls, crowded around the vampire who was alone in his cerebral in-space, the marble firmly in the grip of his shooting fingers, and they were deadly.

For hours, the vampire had enjoyed the rhythm of nickles, dimes, quarters and the surprising appearance of a fifty cent piece. So, what was important to him was the natural roll of the marble, its resistance to friction and the fluidity of its movement; in short, he wanted a winner. The vampire tended toward the literal, and was meticulous in his selection of marbles, so that any vendor who sold him a soiled marble was anathema and dressed down as a worm and worse ... the vampire focused his orbic powers: the large silver coin was already singing around the marble ... it was already his before he released his trigger finger, and it gave him a special glow because he knew he could instill terror in his opponent. Some boys claimed the vampire could bugger a coin with his eyes; all he had to say was Leaping Lizards and a fifty cent moon started waltzing. The only defence was to freak the vampire out, distract him at that split-second when he aimed his murderously accurate marble ... The vampire fixed his gaze ... suffering was the sauce on his lips ... he made a note of the miniscule sphere glowing in the distance ... licked his lips and displayed a killer smile ... giddy, swimming in the haemoglobin of his success ... a quarter ... coins ... line up all the coins ... everybody's ... a quarter was a light pop on the surface of the skin as he drained one marble monger after another ... the first shot was deceptive, close ... a tease ... the second sent the marble and coin into orbit ... the music of the spheres in that ringing coin ... a third was never needed ... the coin sang its sad song:
      SOMEWHERE OVER THE RAINBOW
      SKIES ARE BLUE

A few of the girls laughed, some giggled ... But what excited the exudation of saliva was not silver jangling in the spring air, but the roll of green dollars: marble mongers playing nervously with wads of five, ten and even a rare twenty mixed in with all that green. The germinal capitalist would try to hide the twenty; it was a stiff amount for a ninety-six pound weakling to carry around; he tucked the paper money into a deep pocket and rammed a safety-pin into those heavy bills, securing it to his pant pocket, so that a mugger would have to rip out that pocket with a knife. Every kid playing the fast lane needed a body guard, a pal to stay with him. Green currency had filled the vampire's heart and soul with a hue of bilious envy (I had no jam for the marble game: because once, while I was playing outfield, a blow had sent the softball in my direction and as I ran to catch it I tripped, straining my leg, gimped to the ball, and in the meanwhile all runners headed for home plate. I had earned the hatred of my team mates, and for weeks I left school by the back door, running home because I had lost the game; now, faced with fast marbles, I had come to the conclusion it was better to watch a war than to be in one).

The vampire cared little for the decorative aspect of marbles: green, transparent, speckled silver, gold, blood spots, a few veins rupturing ... the vampire detached himself from the aesthetic ... he was interested in the kill. The dizzy rollers in knee-pants who ran the marble lanes never formed a cartel to keep the vampire at bay; instead, they encouraged the monster to eliminate their competition, thin the ranks and thus allow the strongest to survive, only whetting the killer's appetite as he waited. Each entrepreneur offered a better deal ... more marbles for your money ... a higher value in coinage to challenge one's predatory streak: lured by the challenge of confronting a fifty cent piece ... mere sucklings salivating, because the shinier moon meant a package of Old Gold cigarettes ...

No matter. The vampire had long slender wrists like a gun-fighter, loose as though a bone was missing, and then seconds away before releasing his miracle marble, they stiffened. The proprietor of the lane made his move in the micro-second before firing time. "You fucken fairy," shouted the kid into eternity. "Move yer ass to the girl's line, fruitypie..."

The vampire kept calm as a tombstone.

"Eat shit," shouted the boy. The vampire squatted down. The second was oiled. The killer lived in a closed economy, not unlike a perfect sonnet. He drew back his marble. The jelly defending his coin suffered. The marble supporting the coin shuddered. A psychic shave, nothing more. He let his arm hang loose, squatted, and drew back again, diminishing his prey, reducing the kid's ego to a teensy-weensy marble, a grape seed. The kid muttered a line about Harold. A mug like Harold would stomp on his trigger finger? But we knew Harold was in the vampire's pocket ... bought off, not with marbles but cash, paper cash and coins ... Obviously, Harold had a three-pack-a-day habit, his nicotine weed. Where are the heros when you need them? Over a rainbow, somewhere, or grown up and handing out parking tickets. Harold ...

The vampire knew in his slime of a heart that the kids running the lanes could never keep him away. He had studied the scene like a yellow spider following the heat outline of a smaller insect inside the corolla of a wild orchid ... the prey perfectly outlined in ultra violet...

There was a poisonous substance in him which gave his skin an unhealthy softness and a slight discolouration. His malignant shadow passed over the shooting alleys and the marble elite squeaked. They melted away ... thinning their numbers, their only defense. To quit. He reeled about offering generous odds to anyone who would play a lane. "I'll step back a hundred feet. Look, you dorks, I can't give it away." He had become a leper among the marble set. An animal sound rumbled from his stomach. "Don't be a bunch of fried assholes ... look, you can keep your backsheesh ... Just let me play." Others faded away. The school ground, bustling with pushers, was now empty. The pale gray light of the bully alone with his shadow. They had fled like a biologic organism, an anti-body dissolving before the pathogenic onslaught, and the invading force moved like a pulsation of infected light. Oh, the world is too, too full of shooting lanes, marbles, coin and infected light.

The Invisible Line

Shooting marbles, joy-riding on somebody else's bike, salvaging sidewalk cigarettes: the next thrill was the invisible line game. Evening, a kid winds a black sewing thread around the stem of a door knocker, makes sure the thread is properly secure, pulls the line to see if the mechanism will rise and fall properly, testing it again and again, and then – like a skilful fly casting fisherman – allows loops of slack on the line to fall across the road. The house has an unlit veranda. The street itself is badly lit. He has concealed himself in the darkness. A surge of confidence runs through the child. He stares at a starless sky: the conditions are ideal, pitch blackness, as black as the mischief in a boy's premature soul. Suddenly, he tugs on the line, once, twice ... and waits, his heart pounding, fear pissing through his body.

He cackles to himself. A man opens the door, stares out in disbelief, and closes the door. Only the wind knocking. The wind? There are unusual occurrences in the city. The child pulls on the string. The giant opens the door again. Suspicious, he peers into the street, scratches his head, sniffs the air, and steps onto the veranda. The night is tilted. Moonless. He steps back into the hallway, snapping on the porch light. He touches the doorknob, caresses the thread, seizes the line, carefully lifting it until he scans a direction into the dark, a radio wave from a distant star.

"You little prick," he shouts. He strides across the road, groping for the devil who ruined his supper. "Listen, I'm gonna bust your teeth ..." The kid realizes he hasn't tied onto a doorknob, but the knob of a psychopath who has been waiting a good part of his life to destroy some child in the night. He is stoked, the animal coals burn in his furnace. "I'll kill you ..." The boy is terrified, his young legs carry him away from psychopathic pounding feet. Young legs sprint, fly, as he is racing ahead of his body, white lightning flaring front and back. He hears the gasping giant; every ounce of energy is being burnt away.

I ran so fast I thought my heart would burst. My ribs ached. The marrow went dry. I had run the whole block in a matter of seconds in metaphysical time. I had rung right into the origin of experience, of the relation between things. My protective spirit had entered my limbs and carried me away from the giant toward first principles. Implosion and explosion. There were times I felt him breathing down my neck, his fingers clawing my shoulders. I knew the laneways of the night, zones of shadow, the one loose board in the fence, an eel-hole in the dark. I kept on moving until I knew I was absolutely safe because the lunchbucket crowd didn't play around and were mean at supper time. It was the best run of my life. It sent bolts of electricity through my body, revved my tired spirit. A thought crossed my coarse mind. If I was going to live with the pack I had to be quick on the hoof. Slamming a doorknocker, circa 1948–49, was not just a secret dark highway of sewing thread but a flow of electrons that provided the necessary jag to make me watch my flanks even in the daylight hours. For the doorknocker had hit something more than wood. The man who answered the door (invariably, the person answering the evening call is the man of the manse or mansion) had not only been made a fool of by some street punk, but his castle had been profaned, his master's dinner – prepared so lovingly by his wife the homemaker – lay cold as a frozen rat. Something blew away under his lid, a valve so personal its nearest equivalent is the umbilicus attached to his mother's sacred navel. There he was, the kindest person on the face of the earth, a provider and peaceful monarch to his brood, metamorphosed into a raging killer, a timber wolf licking fresh ink from a croaked rabbit. And nothing is more illusive than safety. Safety's in numbers, not on the run. His pointed shoes hoofed my little bugger ribs, chest and balls. Some numbing feeling from the very roots of my sexual organ traveled directly up to the roof of my feed bag, my gaping mouth. Again, he kicked the lump of meat, me. Caught in a white cocoon of rage, he was actually murdering a child, killing the future, delivering a horrible shit-kicking. Then, a shard of panic-stricken reason prevailed. Self-interest. Fear of consequences. A quiver of remorse.

"Hey kid, get up ... Jeeez, I hope he aint dead." Me, the quivering punk, tiny hands protecting minor manhood, holding my future, groaned.

"Don't hit me mister." That plaintive call of the meek and mild in wild country.

"Here, let me help you, kid. Look, you tell your mom to marry your dad, you hear? And look, you little peckerhead, next time you won't be so lucky, cause if I catch you playing with your little wire

I'm gonna make sure you become a girl, you hear, you little piece of snot."

I shook, and scrubbed a tear from my lights. "Thanks, Mister," I mumbled.

"Yeah, now keep your shit away from my door."

The householder felt good. He suddenly was wearing elevator shoes. He was feeling so wonderful he decided he'd give the child a swift kick in the butt. The boot made contact and the featherweight was lifted off the ground. Such is the art of levitation. I have flown; and staggered down the street where I stopped and leaned against a lamp post. I lit up a cig. The man stared. That sawed-off punk was actually smoking.

"Your mother is a whore," I shouted and darted quick as a switchblade down the lane. The breadearner stared incredulously as though struck by a wave of crud.

"What is the world coming to," he squeaked. "Shitheads. Little shitheads," he said, answering his own question, which gave him pleasure and the confidence to go on in an uncertain world.

When Monsters Smoked

There was a trick you could do with an empty package of Camel cigarettes. You folded the package into several parts, squeezed out the central image of the camel itself and then rolled the parts out until the beast seemed to move across the dunes: the mind drugged by cigarette smoke, drifting. We were blowing smoke behind my house on Major Street. Turning on with the weed, a soaring feeling of confidence, buoyed above the crowd. It took a number of cigarettes to get the habit going. It sizzled sometimes as the smoke shot up the wrong flue, but after a few practice bouts, my soul descended on a spiral. It had a calming affect, although when it went bad for me I would choke, gasp and throw up spots of parakeet blood. I was determined to get the drift of it. I wanted to be like other paranormal people. In those days, everybody wore a cigarette butt in the corner of the mouth. Smokers were the toughest, the meanest, the truest romantics, and if they weren't killing they were loving. They loved and killed before or after the act. Sex seemed an excuse to have a smoke. They sometimes made love without fondling but only staring into each other's button eyes and blowing smoke into each other's faces. This was legal sex. Everybody smoked: detectives, poetroons, cowboys, buffoons, rich dudes, poor Okie folk ... it didn't matter, they had one thing in common: they smoked every damned chance they had: brains, manhood, courage, villainy, what did it matter; facing the last mile on Death Row you smoked, or stepping into the vortex of a cow town you smoked before you smoked your shooting iron.

I smoked Camel, others smoked Black Cat ... which I think was a cigarette for sissies ... You smoked through your nostrils, your mouth, or simultaneously. I loved Frankenstein because he could smoke through his ears. He didn't smoke old Gold ... he only smoked when he was being wired down and shot through with bolts of electricity ... the straps snapped ... his huge chest swelled ...

I was jumping up and down in my seat ... the monster's lips twisted and turned, and then his eyeballs (which weren't his) popped back into their sockets. Frankenstein, it seemed, was an electrical junkey ... somebody you could never trust in an electrical storm, who attracted bolts of lightning as a packinghouse attracts sewer rats, and there he was, the monster with a spike running through the *flat* on the forehead of his skull ... he gurgled words, or rather, he ate sound ... the same sound the mummy made when a deluded scientist unrolled his linen, a regurgitated, half-wormy sound ... urgg ghh murrrr-RRRRRrrr

I stared into the gape of his mouth ... did he have natural teeth though made of spare parts? Who looked at his teeth? ... they were stubs ... they reeked of decay ... The monster jerked against the straps, his huge cement shoes jerked up with the zaps of electricity ... and finally the monster passed out, having climaxed with the last burn, and smoke poured out of his ears ... out of his skin ... His cheap trousers seemed to singe with every electrical fuck in the ear ... and the hands, they were huge ... the good doctor wiped the sweat from his creation's brow ... and the rag steamed ...

"Yes ... yes ... my son ... yes ..." assured the doctor. "You will live ..." and URRRRRG ... gurgled the monster ... urgggh ... and then the monster flaked out. A thought crossed through my mind: supposing I wired the wrong doorknocker and the Monster came to the door ... they would use parts of me to keep the creep together ... nobody screwed around at Dr. Frankenstein's door, only the police captain with one arm who had heard a rumor that the Doctor was rejuvenating the beast who had ripped his arm off before in a vicious encounter. With his steel fist he pounded on the thick oak door. The captain didn't believe in knocking ...

I knew the monster was lurking around the coal bin down in my basement. My mother told me to go down and get potatoes. I was too frightened. The war was still on and there were blackout drills and by some freak coincidence, as soon as I mustered my nerves and went down, the lights suddenly went out. Half my body was steaming in fear. Lights flashed outside the basement window; it seemed my life was flashing away, and goosebumps rashed all over my skin: warm piss, goosebumps and a handful of potatoes, dirt still fresh as the grave ... earth apples ... musty ... Frankenstein's boneyard ...

I was crying and cringing and had anybody said boo I would have jumped out of my mouth. I dashed blindly up the stairs, stopping at the top to puff out my fear. I had gone through dungeons, my imagination yeasting with images of dismemberment ... ripping ... tearing ... choking ... clawing ... but never biting: neither the mummy nor Frankenstein's creation ever bit anybody: they tore off their hands, applied a choking hold, but certainly never bit anybody

... that was for the squeaky vampire who darted around in the early hours of the morning and materialized in a dusty coat, a nocturnal evening dress, a starched white shirt, as though the wearer had been sleeping in a crypt where only moths cleaned up after him. From that day on it was hellish to go down into the basement and sidle past the furnace room, past the hidden presence of the square-headed Frankenstein monster. I was sure he was concealed under the coal. Each shovelful brought me closer to the shuffler. I saw his outline in the flames, his grinding mouth and twisted face. Even monsters love to eat potatoes. He could have been hiding in a burlap bag. I kept away from the spuds and handled the coal shovel gingerly, selecting clumps of coal but not digging deeply into the earth lumps piled to the basement window. I dreaded the coal men lumbering up to the window at the side of the house, dumping sacks of coal onto a shute which ran up to the open window. Hands reached out from the grave, Franky's calloused hands.

 The coal navvy pushed me aside as he swung another bag of coal down the shute, his face covered with grime, and as the man sweated he smeared the dirt across his brow as though he meant to convey how his life was a smear of coal darkness containing the gift of fire. To the householder it was different: it seemed the dirtier he was the more acceptable he seemed; the householder wanted his money's worth and felt elevated viewing a human being who worked with grime ground into his pores. The coal man was doubled over, one hand gripping the nape of the bag, the other supporting his hip and the small of his back, and he gripped the rear end of the bag and hoisted it above his waist, rolling the coal over his back. The coal roared down the shute. The coal man smiled, or at least, he always seemed to smile, and his features were made all hideous by the few blotches of white skin ... advanced leprosy ... and his teeth appeared ominous, and his peep hole eyes. The coal man seemed to love his job, dumping coal without a sign of being disgruntled. A few of the laborers requested a glass of water, lapping the water like sick cats. What disturbed me most about their vocation was their lunch hour ... they munched on a sandwich ... ingested, dust and all, and to top off their meal, they sucked on a cigarette, the quick flow of digestive juices blending with dust and the tar from a Camel or Sweet Cap. Still, none of these actual creatures came close to Frankenstein, whose face – although it appeared clean – had its veneer of sickly light: the filth was on the inside. Frost chilled away at a coalman's face but the dirt acted as a protective layer. It was eerie to see a man with a blackened face not only sweating but exhaling a draft of warm bodily air against the savage nip of winter. They sweated, smearing lines of dirt across their face, and gurgled sounds like the monster, their lungs past repair, dust eating away the linings of their precious lungs ... and then sneezing, dust flying up their nostrils ... and then they laughed.

It was an honest living, more productive than attaching new parts to a monster who had a pair of size twenty shoes and whose head had apparently been flattened by a concrete ironing board. He walked through his dungeons with his hands stiff as wood, his shoulders broad enough to carry two bags of coal. He was at least five ax handles across the back and had bolts on his shoulders and tufts of black hair, transplants as well. The poor dumb bastard tried to form sounds but the only real sound was *MASTER ... master ... master ...* and it made the good doctor's day when his fear of fire singed his very soul, if he had one: *Master master* cried the monster, globs of tears and glue flowing along his jutting jaw.

What a poor dumb clot. He proved to be nothing more than the doctor's evil alter ego, uglier than a toad blowing marsh gas. The coalman had a set of shoes which went crunch crunch crunch melting the snow in their path, but even Frankenstein's shoes belonged to somebody else. Who? *Master Master* ... the mouth formed a harsh sound ... The doctor smiled at his creation. "Yes yes ...my son ... yes ... soon you will have a brain ... yes yes ..." Glue oozed and gurgled out of the monster's mouth at the very mention of a transplanted brain. The monster rammed a finger at the side of his head above his prominent ears: "Brrr aain ...?" Demented, a smile formed around his drooling mouth: the thought of a brain, the delicious watering of the monster's hole of a mouth ...

Another zig-zag of electricity. The operating room was crammed with electrical devices and tubings, electrical panels and giant switches, motors with huge rubber bands and auxiliary engines. The monster, strapped against the table, which was itself on gears and pulleys, strained against his straps. Even the transplanted matt of hair on his flattened head appeared to smoke ... The doctor's assistant, usually a dwarf, tried to restrain the monster, fearing the beast would blow the spark plugs in his cranium. The fury of shattering electricity had brought on psychic orgasm, the monster's eyes blackened, jolts jamming through his body, smoking as well ... and then he lay back, passive ... all he needed was a cigarette ... as the dwarf turned up his bubbly eyes to the doctor, who calmed his twitchy assistant, stroking the poor soul's crooked hump, running his hand over the dwarf's heavy-set eyebrows. *EEeeegor ... all is ready ... soon I will prove that the fools were wrong ... I ... Doctor Frankenstein ... they laughed at me ... I'll show them ... I'll ... who are you staring at ... you fool ... you lump ... dirt ... away with you ... away ... hahahahahaha*

"Yes master, yes ..." Eeeegor squealed, waddling away with his painful hump (at least two sofa cushions high). The hunchback appeared to move sideways, past the coal bin, and he waddled up a flight of concrete stairs. He squealed again, a fiendish cry ... something resembling a laugh, its frostiness melting into the shard of a twitter ... the monster clumps toward the doctor, his hands raised like one in a dream state, those eyes open, those peepers that don't belong to the creature ... planted as seeds of vision, fitted in, played around with, the pulps of eyes ...

There was a huge rabbit-like brain in a jar. Igor fondled the jar, staring like a child at its content ... brain ... brain ... he was transfixed ... "Give me that, you oaf," snarled the doctor, seizing the jar from the hunchback who raised his hands to ward off blows. "No, master ... no ..." The child in Igor had not yet fathomed the gravity of his act: to hold, to fondle, to fabricate, to flush another's brain ... that was to put the hunch on the back of life. That was power. The doctor set the jar on the marble table and connected the circuits. A jag of white thunder illumed the contents of the jar. The monster, supine and sedate, rolled his eyes and suddenly a knowing smile formed on his pale lips.

Unfortunately, there's always a rat's hair in the mills: the brain's former owner was an absolute degenerate, a sociopath, a destructive low-life. After all the soft hum of ozone sucking in a nitrogenous vapor ... glup glup ... and the gases liquefying ... with Igor silently watching in the background, full of hate, assuming that the brain was meant for him (a perverse love triangle here) – the vast bully grunted his approval, popped his eyes and pulled against the straps. Igor screamed, but it was too late, the monster had seized the doctor's wrist ... but it was only a gentle tug, playful ... and Igor, after a touching moment of reconciliation, served as a guide, a procurer for the monster, who huffed and puffed, emitting obscene noises at Igor ...kill kill kill ...

The village folk complained to the one-armed captain, the eyes and ears of the judicial system. Enough was enough. The village inhabitants mobilized for a torch-lit deputation to the castle, a lynching ... there was safety in numbers ... they carried pitchforks, shovels ... knives ... and only the one-armed power-tripping captain was in possession of a long piece of hardware, a revolver. It was curtains for the deadly trio: a frightened Igor hoisted above the heads of the mob ... the doctor stomped to death by the peasants ... and the monster chased into quicksand near the castle ...

"Master," he cried out before he sank into the muck of the subconscious. The castle was torched and everybody but the dead was as happy as vampire bats strung out on a jugular vein. I charged up the basement stairs, my heart thumping. I knew he was down there, that he had pulled himself out of the quicksand. There was a spud in his mouth. He was smoking out of his ears, he was moving across the dunes of my mind leaving huge footprints, and who ... who had worn those huge cement shoes before ...?

"Yank ... You Talk ... No?"

I sank into the plush of the LaSalle theatre, distracted by flickering matches and tributaries of smoke turning in a lightbeam from a film projector. In that cavernous theatre, there was a deep harsh cough, a rattling of an addict's pipes, and he had coughed up a vital glue essential to his personality. The sick man's hacking symphony produced sympathetic coughing from others nearby and in turn, a rippling effect. Cough echoed cough through the whole theatre and the film projector's lightbeam vibrated. I caught the whiff of a sickly sweet smell, tobacco leaf or flesh cured in some wild secret sauce, and the leaf glowed just before it dissolved into a white ash which kept on burning, and noxious fingers of tobacco smoke wormed into the very bowels of that dark theatre, where, having inhaled those greyghosts I slipped into a cloud, and I would have gone on counting white microbes if a hard slap a few seats over hadn't wakened me.

My pre-teen eyes detected a shadow hand moving away from a woman's dress. "You got some wandering hand trouble," a woman hissed at a man who bubbled for a word and squirmed in his seat. "Don't pout," she said, "you're behaving like a child. You're just oversexed," she whispered, "but that's OK." Then the controls snapped. "Bitch, bitch." The voice hovered overhead. "Stop it," she cried. "Shut up," somebody shouted. There were a few boos and then silence absorbed itself. A mood, sullen and perfumed, in a haze of smoke intolerably morbid, took hold as brutal images formed on the silver screen: a yellow foe who appeared to have human features ... a nose and eyes, became vicious and simian ... became sadistic, toxic ... the flesh of the face of the torturer, a Japanese colonel, his teeth pointed like a canine who had just dispatched a jackrabbit.

"You talk Yank ... no?" The sound of the underflesh of the dreaded sublime. Menace: the sexuality of menace. The camera captured the long tapered nails of the colonel, a feral beast, a raging clawish finger ... pointy teeth ... and those slanted eyes almost lidless ... no eyebrows ... eyelashes ... then that tight deformed smile ... contrived ... "Smoke ... Yank ... you like Lucky slike? ...smoke ...

you like?" The blond-haired Yank, heavy-browed and sweating, signalled with a nod. He needed a drag, a smoke. The whole human race needed smoke, was becoming smoke. The colonel suddenly took on the airs of an oily head waiter at a country club (but the Yank had his wrists bound together: not even Houdini could have gotten out of that bondage). The oil can colonel puffed a fag into a glow and passed it gently into the Yank's mouth. The victim tightened a corner of his lips and sucked in smoke, blowing it partly through his nostrils, releasing the rest of the refreshing drag in slow streamers from his mouth. "You talk ..." The Yank spat out a goober. The colonel slapped the cigarette out of the poor devil's mouth. "You got wandering hand trouble," the woman whispered. The yellow toothy creature now forced the most hideous of smiles: its only resemblance ... a gartersnake sucking in a treefrog, that smile of absolute satisfaction as the reptile orgasmed, and then grinned. The yellow blight of a colonel seemed, with every passing millisecond of film space, a degenerate who could eat your mother or, for that matter, everybody's mom. My imagination was alive with all possible features of exciting depravity: wooden splints under warmed up fingers ... a flamed-out blackened eyeball bursting like a sickly grape ... a ruptured eardrum ... But, stangely enough – no dental work. No choppers ...

"You talk ... *yes* ..." The colonel's nostrils flared, sweat beaded on his narrow forehead. He was in heat, a wired-out spider monkey ... only heavier boned, filled out around the biceps ... and his terrible fingers had grown in length ... they itched to rend something decent ... tapered like chopsticks, delicate ... The colonel struck a match with one long finger nail and in the flare of the flame I saw his face, it too seemed tapered ... and then the flame went out, and his hand disappeared as the man with hand trouble plunged under the woman's dress in the sepulchral light of the movie house. Her hand was on his ... my eyes shifted from the torture on the silver screen to the huffing of the pair ... a rising tide of breath, abruptive, a ripple of coughing, the sweet sickly smell of cheap perfume and the shave lotion of lust at the movies, a little lowlife high on sexual energy and resigned to a sad fate, the result of the heat ... a secret emission ... The friction of thighs pressed together ... a hot tongue in her cool ear ... she, biting on his lip. "Shut up." The slap that came was from the colonel. He struck the Yank with a blow that sent his blond head banging on the floor. Two stout, very short Japanese guards picked the man up. Everybody was sweating. The tortured soldier was clearly dead ... his face blotched with burns ... but water was poured into his mouth. The colonel stopped smiling ... smoking flesh in the air ... acrid smoke ... groans ... the Yank was a pool of stagnant water ... a muted voice trapped inside a frozen cry ... (A small dog struck by a car on the crescent across from the theatre: a sickening thud, a high squeal and the dying dog crawling slowly to the side of the curb to die. Some kids trying to comfort it as it lay with pathetic soft eyes staring ... a school girl sobbing while she supported the animal on her small lap. A boy had run to get someone but it was too late ... blood spurted out of its mouth and nostrils, the eyes getting colder ... the animal gazed and I saw a glassy expression, a fixed glaze that had the coldness of marble, a look locked on nothingness, the look of one resigned to dying that said everything that had to be said about suffering: even as life left the dog, it struggled for every second of intake until the final frost chilled its vital organs. The dog taught me more than all the would-be miniscule Napoleans who entered the pores of pedagogy. I had learned to read and write but had I learned to live? The beast, pitying himself in his canine soul, was weeping for us. Soon some janitor would wrap the dog in an oily blanket and dump the dead. But only children stood by the curb during the dying. Perhaps larger folk couldn't show their feelings on a short sleeve? A trickle of blood ... a dead dog. A dead dog, a dead heart, a dead dead thing. I seemed never slated for luck but was sensitive to its touch, the brush of a falling leaf on a November night. I felt more drained than the passing dog as I stared, locked in wonder, at the colonel, that overachiever. His English was broken but it was sufficient, so that like a good surgeon he smiled ...).

"I think you talk, no ..."

The colonel believed in his cause just as the dog desperately hung on to life. Belief is power, the true believer is the thug in uniform, whether soutane or sweaty sergeant's jackboots. I didn't believe in anything. I played the game on their terms. The dog couldn't fathom the rules: crossing the street was like Russian roulette. No more tail-wagging. The boy friend puffed on a cigarette. He believed in getting it off, a little tail, "The bitch," getting rid of heat.

"You talk, Yank ... no?" The Yank spit a goober of glue at his tormentor. The dog's glue was left a little while on the curb. The following flick had a mummy in it who struggled in a world of bandages. That bandaged freak was really angry, and no wonder: he was doomed to stand at attention for four thousand years. Chick's perfect student.

Mummies & More

In the twenties, Cantor Rosenblatt (no relation) had a voice comparable to Caruso's. An orthodox Jew, Yossele Rosenblatt, refused to shave his beard and conform, and so – unacceptable to Tinsel Land – the Hollywood moguls gave up on him. They cut him adrift in his own dreams. Nevertheless, he went on singing his heart out to a more appreciative audience. The Chaliapin of the synagogues. So the legend went in Yiddish films, his spectral image staring into his dressing room mirror, his beard white as his pallid shocked expression. It appeared he was on the verge of surrendering his soul ... distraught, clutching a telegram, or is it a letter, an ultimate tear jerker, and I couldn't stop crying, aching for the Cantor. The dialogue was entirely in Yiddish, produced by an American Yiddish film company. A number of other sentimental Yiddish flicks – sweet, bitter and blended with comedy – made the rounds in the forties at the LaSalle. Coming out of the theatre one day, I saw a man had been struck by a car and he lay still just like that dog. A crowd stared back. Locked on the nothingness that hung between them. Without trying to see who the dying man was, I dashed home to tell my mother that dad had been struck by a car. She dropped what she was doing and dashed down the street. Pushing her way through the crowd, she discovered the person lying still on the road was somebody else and was so relieved that my father was still alive that she forgot to smack me for scaring the wits out of her. I was prone to accident. There seemed to be accidents wherever I was ... a melancholic atmosphere feeding reels of silver melancholia to a hungry audience, or schools filled with student dread and fear of authority, all amounting to manic affairs and mental scars. A dead dog symbolized this phase of my life: trusting only a few friends and a dead dog. Perhaps the accident victim had been at the LaSalle, and depressed by the newsreels, had wandered into the traffic, blinded by a veil of tears.

Certainly a veil of fear had enveloped Jewry, even as I saw Cantor Rosenblatt absorbed in gloom, studying his features in the mirror. My father had come to Canada from Lodz, Poland. He had worked at menial jobs until he scraped together savings enough to bring my mother over in 1932. My uncle Nathan, who eked out a meagre living from his small fish store on Baldwin street (an enterprise he founded in 1926 and which sadly folded when he died in 1956) had assisted my parents as they'd settled down in their new life. Despite the horrors of the Great Depression, life in Canada, according to my father, was preferable to anti-Semitic Poland.

But hatred works by degrees. The political climate was inhospitable to immigrants competing with native sons for employment; as in Europe, anti-Semitism found fertile soil in the impoverished national psyche. Poverty doesn't link people together in mutual support; it agglutinates hatred, hatreds like barnacles attaching, each to another. Native eyes are directed at a scapegoat, a minority, and not at the ruling classes who are able to distance themselves from hateful fermentation. The poor hate the poor and the poorer you are the more you're hated. The mob, striving for social mobility, pins the poverty stricken to the wall ... they fear being dragged down into the furnace room, their spare parts used to build up moral inferiors ... those chosen pieces attached to lepers, who serve the total monster (*Master, master*) the system itself: it is a culture of obsolescence, of spare parts and there is a perverse love affair here. Immutable, the blight grows and flourishes. Nutured by perversity, it regenerates itself.

My parents settled in Kensington Lane a year before I was born. The rented cold water flat had only one water tap and a sink in the bathroom. They paid twelve dollars a month for the slum and often when I go past that laneway, I wonder where it was, exactly. Father earned two dollars a day when he worked. Like millions of people my parents suffered deprivation during the Depression and yet – because I was over-protected – I have no memory of hardships. Staring into a family photo, circa 1936, I see a fat child in short pants, dour between my smiling parents. I am seated on a family table which is as polished and bright as I am melancholic, peeping out at a world making faces at me.

My parents moved out of Kensington Lane and settled on Markham Street, not far from the market. It is the house I recall during the war years: sirens wailing in the city ... practice drills ... people hurrying home although no bombs rained down ... but there was fear itself, and it invaded the psyche of a ten-year-old who would soon learn the dreadful truth about the Final Solution on that dancing beam of light in the La Salle theatre. It happened at a regular Saturday matinée. That devastating feature changed my life in a matter of twenty minutes. The regular movie had ended, some inane flick titled the Curse of the Mummy, which had scared the juices out of me, and I was dry, or so I thought. The sights and sounds of snapping linen as the stiffs broke free from their bondage and bandages had had me leaping from my seat, and then had left me limp.

When this regular silver screen delight ended, the ushers told the kids that they had to leave. They waved droves of kids toward the exits. What was next on the Bill was for a mature audience only, and ushers flashed their flashlights, bellowed out orders, looked under seats and moved us all in single files down the aisles. Teachers, ushers, single files. I ducked into the washroom to hide. I had no intention of missing Mickey Mouse with teeth or Minnie with tits.

The silence in the half-empty theatre gave it another dimension: the other side of the grave. A booming voice described the death camp survivors just liberated by the advancing British forces. Cadaveric sights flashed across the screen. I felt an icy presence, a chill: those hills of shoes scattered about immediately grabbed my lights ... I spotted a child's shoe, and then many children's shoes ... tons of sorrowful shoes ... stark black and white ... hills of corpses suddenly appeared to be moving ... a harvest of naked death ... skeletal dunes, twisted ... their bones falling apart ... skulls ... spare legs that had no flesh ... mounds of dead ... starved beyond death itself... their eyes bulging in disbelief... their mouths open... screaming ... at whom? ... at the young Tommies, their young faces pallid, soldiers covering their faces ... the acid sweet smell of rotting hands, hearts ... sprawled ... flung ... a child ...a rhythmic flow of death ... the dead screaming in flecks of silver before my eyes ... as though static electricity had become the larvae of death ... but still, there were those among the dead who were reaching out at the living ...

The Tommies delicately carried a few skeletal children, their dangling chalky limbs moving ... and the flesh on their limbs ... what flesh? ... there didn't seem to be any ... flesh ...white loose skin ... a skein of terror ... the gritty quality of the film gave the elements a life form of their own ... a rain had fallen, giving the film a feeling there was dew clinging to it ... a wash to the permanent stain ... and now the whole mongrelized feeling was present ... a montage of super death ... the machinery, fresh ... no time to move the evidence, the technology that went into this industry of death, fillings become bars of gold ... hair becomes mattress stuffing ... the doors of the ovens ... swung open ... white mounds ... the crematoriums for turning corpses into potash ... half-baked, hair still on the skulls in the narrow ovens ... Tommy groomed to a T, held a delicate handkerchief to his nose and explored the dead. A frightened gleam appeared in his eye, his face without emotion, his pistol drawn, leading a rigid SS officer dressed smartly in leather into the building. In the next shot, the officer had the glazed look of a marble.

I left the theatre before the newsreel ended. There wasn't anybody in the lobby. I had moved ahead of the crowd. In the street I felt suddenly strange, like a moth stormed by sunlight; I drifted, as a ghost would drift away from the surface of the planet.

The Friendly Giant

There lived a friendly giant on Major street who kids loved to taunt and throw stones at, and they made vicious comments when he lumbered by, his blue eyes fixed upon an imaginary horizon that always existed, even when blanketing snow fell on the street. The children followed Harvey, a few demons tugging at his coat, pulling his suspenders. They threw snowballs at him, striking the side of his face, or a fattened snowball struck him full in the face, eliciting a large collective laugh as Harvey wiped away the shame and managed to smile while the children continued pelting him. Harvey reeled from the blows. He appeared cursed. Even as he pleaded in his own sheepish way, "Please don't hurt me ... you are bad boys," the mobs followed him down the street. The trouble was, Harvey didn't have a mean bone in his childish psyche. He wouldn't have harmed a blowfly feasting on his blood. Harvey, the poor giant, had wept many times surrounded by street gangs. He became their surrogate monster, their substitute Frankenstein creation ... and while it is true he didn't have a spike through his forehead, each foot deliberated as it hit the pavement, as though his shoes were casements of cement.

Actually, Harvey and the monster had few things in common. Frankenstein never stopped at a neighbor's picket fence and fondled a marigold or sniffed the hollyhocks, nor did he feel depressed about a damaged Monarch or sigh as the sun struck a huge sunflower. He marvelled at the sunflower's construction, itself a lost plant soul manured in sheep shit – perhaps a living thoughtful plant in prayer? You would have thought so watching Harvey lean over the fence, stretching his neck to get a closer look. He always appeared to pull his neck out to study plants, people, and to gaze directly ahead, smiling at a horizon none of us ever saw. I liked Harvey: he appeared happy but somehow sad on the inside. In short, he was in constant pain and more miserable than me. Here was someone I could set my compass at, remind every particle groaning in me that there was someone sadder. I gazed on him as some people spy on birds. I followed him, and even years later – in the fifties – I chanced to find that he had become my neighbor in another part of the city. I began to hate the children who tormented Harvey, and yet I had become as helpless as he. When I made any defensive gestures on his behalf, they relentlessly showed how cruel they could be: someone zipped behind him and another suddenly darted in front, while a third evil creature shoved at his middle, and back he fell, three hundred and some odd pounds striking the pavement, wailing, crying, pleading, reaching desperately, calling for his mother and father. Sprawling on the sidewalk, all seven feet of him, Harvey rolled his eyes like a wounded animal slugged on the crown with a sledgehammer. He tried to lift himself and fell back sobbing while I ran to get the neighbors.

Harvey, in his thirties, not only suffered from giantism and slurred speech, but he had an eight-year-old mind locked away inside a huge skull. It sickened me to see him sliding on ice while, in his vulnerable state, some kids tied his shoelaces together. The neighbors, although shocked by Harvey's mistreatment, somehow never managed to catch any of the rascals. They accepted his sad state of affairs as a condition of life; nothing could be done to lessen the plight of the giant. Every morning, Harvey's dad fastened his suspenders to his huge pair of pants and stood on a chair to straighten Harvey's threads, his shirt and tie, and sent him out for a walk in the world, his smile concealing a hurt. It was Harvey's defence. He refused to show he was hurt. His huge shoes rose and fell with a heavy thud. He stared at the sky, at that horizon. It was a fixed blue stare, and he said nothing, as though his mouth were closed by ice.

On the Street of Dreams

There is something pathetic about a brain in a jar, a rabbit brain with long pink stem exposed, floating in formaldehyde, so human that I ponder the relationship between man and rodents. Feelings are sometimes locked away in special jars. Should feelings grow, they soon break through their glass compartments, spreading their filaments into the light, feeling the air. This is the human dream, never to return to a jar.

Again, I thought of the monster's brain afloat in a jar, and the good doctor Frankenstein studying the shape. Our films and flicks were prophetic, acidic in their acuity. The monster was on the operating slab, the top of his flattened head sawed off, the flap pulled back. It was up to the doctor to replace what once resided under the monster's roof. The doctor fixed his gaze on an adjoining jar. It, too, had a brain in it, to be deposited in the monster's cranial chapel, attached to its blood vessels, connected to the correct tributaries. The doctor deposited that new brain as gingerly as an orchid lover returning a rare orchid to a rock garden crevice, delicately planting the fragile plant, pressing the rootlets beneath precious earth and moss ... The doctor wore his special surgical gloves that came up to the elbows; after the doctor had attached the whole neurological system, there was blood on the spotless surgical white apron. That brain wasn't just a mortal brain, an ordinary organ, but a child entity. There was something keenly metaphysical about the operation; there couldn't be birth without blood, denoting that blood was needed to build a new order of man. This stretched the optic nerves of the imagination. The doctor had conveyed the new brain to his creation's throne room, and reason was then to prevail. The doctor studied his handiwork by staring deeply into the eyes of his creation. He passed a beam of light across the monster's eyes and they flickered, acknowledging the master's presence ... and the master was the light of the universe, the monster's savior. The monster gurgled, spittle running out of a corner of his mouth, his chest heaved and sounds issued from his distorted mouth. He was feeling joy. "My boy ... my boy," the doctor cried, his heart ringing with pride, with affection, for here, in His own image ... So it begins, again and again ...

But I was curious about the gloves, the way the doctor held them up to the vibrating light bulbs, enveloped in a gaseous light. An antiseptic light had killed the harmful bacteria. Another bolt of light passed through the monster's system and smoke poured out of his ears. The doctor screamed out to Igor to lower the voltage; it was killing his child. A few soft flashes followed and the monster sighed on the slab, falling into a deep sleep. The doctor wiped the globules of sweat from his child monster's forehead. "Sleep, my boy," the healer muttered. The child falls into a fog, a smile forms on his lips. Even Igor was smiling at the child, the super child. Igor, his face twisted, for he was the doctor's conscience, growled after the doctor had stitched the scalp, smoothed down the hair piece ... The doctor slapped Igor, but it was a loving slap, one the dwarf appreciated as he kissed the doctor's ungloved fingers. Then, swinging his humped back and twisting a lame foot, he turned to leave, stopping at the foot of the stairs to ponder the monster lying on the slab. Had the doctor used the brain of a butcher lad, a cunning merchant ... or possibly the grey protoplasm of a clergyman? Igor had been so skillful in acquiring fresh cadavers that he had ventured out during the day. He was trying to overwhelm his master with a selection of stiffs. The Boss hadn't the heart to scold him; only to rap him across his sloped shoulders, or perhaps he would have to whip him, except this worried the doctor. Igor was begging for attention, even a whipping.

He lifted the monster's eyelid and drew a light beam across that naked eyeball. He gloated, a portent of things to come, a sutured, transplant future, but none will have the good doctor's metaphysical bent akin to shamanism ... there will be heart, kidney, liver, and other organ transplants enough, but it was the throne room of man, psychic humankind, the last frontier with which he had begun ... with all the passions of a major poet. It staggered the fragile mind. The doctor wasn't merely gutting a human chicken, one of the town's petit bourgeois merchants and craftsmen, removing a kidney stone from the decorative bird. He was retreading the New Man: the Marxist New Prol ... The New Aryan Mensch ... Somewhere in the dismal future, a surgeon gloats, inspired by this twisted medical poetry; and to think that the good doctor's only opposition was the illiterate townsfolk led by a police captain whose prong of a prosthesis was a steel hook formed into a question mark, and all intimacy and loyalty resided in the hump of a deformed dwarf. Did the righteous townfolk, killing the murderous dream of re-creation and perfection ... killing the optimism inherent in the healing doctor's savage indifference to the lives he intended to dignify ... did they bring home their work during rush hour ... a shrunken human head ... a pickled hump ... a brain in a jar to amuse a child ...?

Pea-Brained

I inserted a dry green pea into my ear. I don't know why I thought the little green bean would alleviate the throbbing in my ear, and as I plumb memory for a reason I find myself slipping back into the bog of time just like that wee bean which sank down into the ear canal. It vanished, and suffice to say, I wasn't a very bright twelve-year-old. Still, self preservation illumed in my brain and I managed to blurt out what had happened to my father, who remained as calm as a rock. He sighed a little, muttered something inaudible, and decided to escort me by streetcar to Sick Children's Hospital. I said nothing during the ride and father was silent. I could feel the pregnant pressures of the bean which had come to rest at the bottom of the chasm above the eardrum. My ear had become alive, a rootlet in the bean desired to break out of its shell. There was a sprout of a plant there and after a while it seemed natural that the green pea should be there. Another advantage was that Crunchdale could shout at me and it would be nothing more than a whisper working around the wee boulder. I entertained a few other light fantasies as I waited in the corridor with kids and their parents. Nobody asked me what I was doing there, and if they did, how could I tell them I had had an earache and there was this pea which had slipped down ... and the ear seemed to have accepted the stranger.

A serious young intern positioned me on my side on the narrow table and told me not to move as he forced a pencil flashlight very gently into the outer ear. He tried probing the ear with a delicate steel instrument and then decided upon another, slimmer instrument. As he poked around, trying to find the bean, I felt the heat of the light burning my earlobe. Finally, he found the bean and forced it half-way to the surface. He reached for a tweaser and opened the insect-like jaws.

He held the offensive bean up to my father in triumph. No one asked why I had placed the bean in the vase of my ear. The prize appeared as fresh as it had been before planting. None of the greenness had been lost; there was only a slight waxy sediment and gloss.

What fascinated me was the thin light beam from the intern's pencil flashlight. It was more advanced than Doctor Frankenstein's special tube light and had I been in Frankenstein's hands I would have had a head transplant (the monster's grey eyes flickered, the doctor realized his creation had been connected ... a cerebral circuit was working without chance of a blowout ... even the heavy eyebrows moved as the light registered on the brain and the monster seemed pleased, licking his lips, so the doctor played a beam across the monster's line of vision and again the creature acknowledged the light by breaking into a hideous smile ... the same grimace as later, when directed by a defective and deteriorating brain, he stumbled into bubbling mud and the fiendishly deranged mob watched Frankenstein's baby take a final bubble bath in the hot mud ... a symbolic hand grasping the living air, forming into a fist as the monster slid beneath the muck into my subconscious, turning like a maggot ... but he will surface again, since you can't keep the implant down for long ...). The intern kept the pea; the canal was clear, and I could hear the monster's howl as he sank in the bog, and Harvey's cry of bewildered pain, and the pain of children being strapped by Miss Plover ... but my father said nothing, staring as we rode home on the streetcar at his own horizon line that I could not see, opening and closing his hand on the living air.

Horse Meat

A horse is loyal, but when the creature can't haul his weight he's shuffled off to the glue factory. Loyalty zips out through Death's round door. Connoisseurs who've taken their brood to the circus to watch the fine-lined creatures prance, their tails tied in a bun and heads held high, say the servant's meat – all the specialty cuts from equine carnage laid out in specially licensed shops – tastes sweet. The poor horse, a purely herbivorous creature, also serves in death, but in life a pony loves a fresh carrot with blackened soil on its tapered carotene body, and the stallion loves a sugar cube and neighs its vital thanks, a love purer than man's as he drags a junk wagon or a cart heaped with voluptuous vegetables around a corner.

    I remember the old peddlers in the forties leading their four-legged companions down our street. During the heat of a summer's day, kids offered the nag a sugar cube or an apple, and the long yellow nicotine-colored teeth chomped on our tidbits, our offerings. Then, the peddler shooed us away, complaining we had molested his precious and boon companion. The peddlers have disappeared; chrome-plated horseless machines have taken over, but I remember when an old bearded peddler lifted me up on his nag's back and I cried when I stared down at the ground and kicked the creature in the flanks with my baby shoes. I'm sure the old horse smiled. They always seemed to smile in their garage-style barns, the dirt floors strewn with hay. How they survived the winters I'll never know. I don't recall wood burning stoves, although there were plenty of horse blankets and an old man's affection. A deep bond existed between horse and peddler, a miserable pair broken by a deadening vocation, existing on the small change of life, making the street rounds searching for broken shoes, a soiled jacket, a tie, an ironing board, a frayed lamp shade. It was a cycle: the poor feeding on the poor. Horse and master, a visible minority verbally abused by street toughs. Shunned, both horse and peddler were considered – by those riding the wheels of social mobility – fossilized ghetto figures.

    So, horse and wagon have disappeared, along with trails of

steaming golden apples glittering in the afternoon sun. They were scooped up for fertilizer by street folk to increase the voltage of plants in a front garden. I stared at the supernatural glow in the faces of sunflowers and marvelled at how that magical dung sustained those wild blooms. Today, the only horse balls are those dropped by the stallions of city cossacks down at city hall square, and no sunflowers loom up in the minds of cops.

There was a happier time when a horse had his or her favorite watering hole. I remember a coppery fountain on the southwest corner of Spadina and College, the fountain's green skin of floral patterns fringing its surface. The artisan who designed the fountain had a sense of humor: there was a cherubic figure who greeted the snouts of horses with a jet of cold water and a small nude comedian peed in an arc and many a kid leaped under it, frolicking in the maw of the fountain during a July heat wave. Until nudged by a horse, he retreated with the peddler shouting that the sanctity of the fountain had been profaned by a pint-sized hooligan. To make his point, the man waved his horse whip above his head.

To this day, I can't stand the thought of using glue. I instantly associate it with horses who've been sold out. What would Roy say about glue and horses. He'd never have put Trigger on a conveyor belt. To hell with mucilage made from horses ... the viscous stuff sickens me. I smell horse in the glue bottle, and suspect horse glue on a postage stamp. How would you like to lick old Dobbin goodbye? They've made ashtrays out of the knuckles of elephants and shoes from grinning alligators, and the testacles of tigers are dried and ground to powder for septuagenarians hoping to get it up one last time in the Far East. Nothing is sacred, not even human skin, which provides a delicate pinkish hue for lampshades, so rosy a light for concentrated romance. Pain and leather conjoin. An old prole of a drayhorse is offered a few sugary rocks, or a carrot (the animal's pacifist heart clouds its judgement) and other sweetened tidbits, so he ambles through a maze of stalls wiped clean of blood and there's muzak in the air: a smart marching tune calms the creature into thinking he (or she) is at a horse fair out in the country, or back home. Even the air has the tang of the freshest alfalfa and sweet grass, a special brand, or type, reserved for the thoroughbred winner.

The cynical engineer has contrived an intricate plan. The animal moves through stalls of friendly colors, and neighs: a few have been painted symbologically – a pleasing bovinish landscape ... a peaceable kingdom that would have delighted Rousseau ... bovine figures lurking in high grass, a brown squirrel cleverly pawing a chestnut ... a colbalt-hued bird on a branch and a lamb asleep at the foot of a shepherd wearing a candy striped robe ... loud bulbous blooms ... stamens licking exaggerated bumblebees ... and a spring peeper on the face of a leaf on a branch ...

An innocent intellect gestates in the retired drayhorse. His herbivorian heart swells. Grunting, he has discovered paradise, lulled into the maw of a delicately crafted Bucolics; in short, he is a primitive Virgil absorbed in an elegiac atmosphere, and he deliberates on tonalities intermingling in the paintings. Already anaesthetized through wave lengths of color, the horse heads toward a stall in which a hole has been cut to fit an equine head. The beast views a carrot tree awaiting him through the hole. It is the pièce d'ocassion. The retired prole pushes his head and neck through the hole, deducing through some inverted logic that it has been especially cut by his master to accommodate him. He not only views hyped-up carrot trees but an apple tree with its low boughs burgeoning with lusty apples. Of course, it's too damned good to be true, and there's something out of place with the carrot tree; by now, the animal has remembered that carrots don't grow on trees. Locked in the feed hole, he will be spared the mental arithmetic used exclusively by horses – that carrot tree and apple fixation don't amount to heaven – they are only a clever joke as the cynic's heavenly moment arrives. He releases the trigger of his hammer gun. There's a sickening thud as a steel rod slices through the horse's skull, shooting the brains out at the other end, and sometimes a puzzled seed of a brown eye. Another workman moves with a precise mechanical rhythm, ax in hand. He neatly cleaves off the head at the neck. The creature's magnificent head flies into a basket (entitled The Last Sure Bet by the boys in the slaughterhouse). Not to be outdone by this clean single rhythm, he is joined by another burly workman draped in a plastic yellow jacket and in boots like chestwaders any angler would be pleased to wear at a trout stream. The man slashes open the horse's belly (the hole in the stall has mechanically enlarged itself and another workman has shoved the decapitated beast back, receiving a splash of blood pumped from the still active heart) and the guts slide out onto the floor ... the material oozes on the phony green carpet that simulated a mossy grass to the passing horse on its way to the round hole, the Grim Reaper's entrance to his condominium ...

The belly-ripper is joined by a clean-up man who shoves a long gloved hand into the interior of the belly, pulling out any stubborn organs and entrails; in fact, he has become a specialist, a poetic mortis of gastro-intestinal delicacies ... and this belly brigade works fast and furiously. They hose out the innards, wash down the horse, clean up the blood on the phony grass floor with a high pressure hose ... and then, falling on their knees, they scrub the blood out with tungsten brushes, oblivious to a huge hook and chain lifting the horse's carcass up and along a track toward a steamy vat where the cadaver is dumped. It is the final cooking pot, and the boys love to jazz a kid new on the job by plucking an eyeball from the horse's quiet socket. "Go on, make a man out of you ... come on punk, suck on this eyeball ..." The testacles and the immense member of the horse – which has released a streak of violence – wag by: "Boy, if the old lady could see that one. Jeeze, I wish I wuz that well hung ... Hey kid ... don't you wish you had a stick like that ... what a porker ..."

The kid throws up his breakfast. He'll learn it's best to eat after the work shift. Still, the idea of a horse fills your belly with bile and creeps up into your throat at two in the morning and then slides back into your lungs until you think you are going to choke to death. It's a hard life. But your friends say you're suffering overactive guilt anxiety and you keep on trucking because you're not a quitter and there are good benefits ... health plans ... free dental care ... a pension and other fringe benefits that make up cradle-to-the-grave security. You may even advance to overseer of the big glue pot, the soup where bits and pieces of horse flesh fall apart from the bones ... the soup having the consistency of good black beans, but the odd joker will point to an eyeball floating and quip that the dark vision consumes in consommé.

The soup gives off a sickening smell, sweet, and sometimes acidy, with traces of sulphur and shit (legend has it, depending on who lips the narrative, that a few lads fell into the pot while stoned on super-grass, and the morning crew found them floating, cooked inside and out, the flesh shedding, the human bones joining the horse frames at the bottom: the more poetic amongst the staff thought that the soup might serve as a sacrificial well ... maybe bring in a hooker off the street ... maybe a show before the soup is served, a little mooning before the moon goddess is placated). The kid backs away like a maggot who has just smelled clean meat, squeezing his hand over his mouth trying to keep from wretching on the cleaned green ... and somewhere arrows are singing out in space ... but the punk hasn't heard of the Battle of Hastings, about dry ice evaporating: what does the punk know about Harold and the arrowhead in his eyeball ... Only the last chilling cry reaches him just before the thud of the rod crushes the skull of another animal. The triggerman doesn't like anybody crowding his job, infringing on his relationship with the horse. Nobody joins the triggerman for a beer after work. And the triggerman doesn't care; like the hangman, he feels he has a mission as Keeper Of The Glue. Sometimes the triggerman complains about the music; he doesn't know tone from a bone. He hates sound, any sweet sound. He loves only the spit and rattle of his gun, the way it vibrates in his hand. He loves the closed expression of the dead horse. The triggerman loves horses. He has a collection of horse paintings on velvet; the masterpiece was painted by a woman who had no hands, claiming she painted it with a brush clamped between her teeth ...

The muzak continues. A red light flares. The triggerman is ever alert for the approach of a horse. All the time he is thinking about hyper space; he knows there's a triggerman or woman for everybody, and if he gets it, will he feel pain? Do any of us feel pain after we die? His clammy finger squeezes the trigger. He doesn't hear the *bpop* of the rod singing in the horse's skull. Meat. And more meat. The triggerman laughs, and he can't stop laughing. Laughter has taken possession of him. It's finally come to that. Frost has formed around his mouth. He could be dead, but his mind goes on humming and laughter becomes his cosmic wisdom. His mouth is open as though with each squeeze of the trigger he lost his cherry ... he is virgin death, alive on black velvet. A horse neighs among the painted crocuses. Those floating eyes, the pollen of what we know, what's been seen. This Way To The Crocuses Ladies And Gentlemen.

Is there freezer burn out in space?

A Few Hors D'Oeuvres

A gelatinous impure protein, my thoughts drop, viscous drop by drop. History itself is glue. Who remembers horses or people? We affirm ouselves by remembering the dead. A gifted spider catches a fly on its net, shuffles across the adhesive web with its anti-glue feet, and then back with fresh meat. He is the future. A fish with a jaw only a fishy mother could love aches for a string of flesh. That working jaw is the future. Everbody's crying for meat balls in a nation that loves its meat. You need meat every day of your life. The tartare. Meat and more meat. But glue doesn't always have to be equated with death. Glue has joined broken bones, closed a fissure in the heart muscle, and soon there will be a compound to build up your rotting teeth, a dental glue, and your kin can fill up on sugars ... Still, meat is the matter of the moment ... How do those hooves break down in the pot ... What's the mean temperature for breaking down fat? Hooves and other spare parts sink down ... but those vapors ... you inhale a sirloin of horse and it floats across your mind ... what other endless possibilities are there, afloat in your mind?

Chick raises several fingers on his left hand: the horses prance counterclockwise. They move around the stalls several times, and then as if by magic they stop, raise their legs and pose until Chick drops his hand ... They neigh ... the equestrian set love it ... This time, Chick tries the right hand, clockwise; the animals move in perfect formation ... A blood-sucking horsefly of thought sings by my eyes, blood still ripe on its miniscule mouth. There's an arrow lodged in the horsefly's eye. Whose been sticking pins into flies? Chick gives one of the horses a detention. The prancer screwed up on the run. The animal drops a fresh bun on the floor. It steams up at Chick who takes no notice. Chick has seen worse on the floor. He has warned the creature that if it screws up again then it's the glue house, no appeals, just glue ... a bookbinder's glue, the strongest ... glue to put a spelling primer together ... glue to keep the pages alive ... pages about the Empire ... Saxons ... History ...

I ask myself, would Hoppy have led his horse to a final country club? Would he have stood by while some dirty bushwacker blew away his *hoss*? Nobody fucks with Hoppy or his hoss, nobody. Hoppy's horse couldn't count to ten like Roy's *Trigger* ... no, Hoppy's horses were ordinary sod clompers, but they trusted Hoppy ... and for good reason ... Even if the slaughterhouse looked like a country club with smells of fresh hay, clover, carrots ... Hoppy would have smelled a trap ... it wouldn't have made any difference if there was a fat sign slung across the Double T Rancho Abattoir: *Horses welcome ... This Is Your Love Boat ...*

Hoppy, his sprawling white hat jumping on his roof, reaches for his pearl-handled silver revolver, the one that snorts lead, and raises the iron piece to the hoss dealer who doesn't have a tool the size of Hoppy's ... Hoppy smells a glue field, a trap. "Hey, stranger, you keep away you hear ... you aint gonna get my pal ... no, me and him, why we's ... family." The fat dude hoss collector is gurgling. He doesn't want to cross Hoppy or slap leather with the white-haired gentleman in his black outfit. "Don't fuck with Hoppy, mister, otherwise you'll be whistling through your eyebrows. What Hoppy's talking about, you see, is loyalty." Now there's a rum word.

The hoss collector backs away leaving a trail of cowardly shit. Hoppy's eyes would have melted the fruit bar. Hoppy could kill with his eyes. A bushwacker ran before he'd cross eyes with Hoppy. Happy trails for Hoppy, transcendental Hoppy shooting through time ... Hoppy had his hoss and they kept each other warm along those trails, both with an eye open for vultures behind basalt ... I wonder if Hoppy had a gelded hoss, or maybe he let his pal keep his nuts? And what unknown horse is out there now with his hoss seed?

Anyway, Hoppy wouldn't let his plain old hoss down into the soup.

Trigger was another matter: he was a smart horse. You'd swear that horse had a PhD, a brain inside the animal's proud head. Didn't Trigger count to a thousand and then divide it by ... and break it down into decimal points ... sure, I'm putting too much glue on this smart animal but the horse had a habit of listening very carefully, and Roy knew it ... Why did you stuff him Roy? Cause he was smart? Cause you had to have him around the house? Does he still do his dignified trick in the after hours of your life?

Trigg could also smell danger along the trail. He saved the boss's life, and when the bushwacker missed, then Roy popped the sucker with a long silver iron piece. I am no pacifist, though the only pea in my shooter ended up in my ear. What I'm talking about is loyalty among some lonesome loonies ... tall in the saddle like Roy, defensive fighters, like rattlesnakes, and just as quick, who always gave warning before they struck ... fair is fair if you invade the lair ... there are, in life you see, these three: the lone loonies, the bushwackers, and the mechanical triggermen who love black velvet ...

Take the Lone Ranger, that egotistical masked loonie. The smiling clean-shaven honkie who was always ordering his Indian factotum around ... and Tonto seemed to be the perfect ass-licker who had this awful habit of saying, Yes Kimisabeeeee, No Kimisabeeeee ... He and the masked freako always rode off into the sunset. There seemed something odd about the two, something horridly unnatural ... two smart riders who rode high ho Silver away ... the masked lunatic, the one with the sticky smile, perched on a white horse. Crime was in the air like love:

"Hey, Tonto, let's stop for some chow."

"No time Kimisabe, we go ... Tombstone ... yes?"

"You're right, Tonto, as usual ..."

So, Tonto and his honky friend rode the trails to Tombstone. I remember how all the townsfolk were suspicious of a *masked man* who'd lose his nuts before he'd take off his blinkers. Nobody fucked with the masked man, nobody molested the flanks of his horse ... the *masked man* had to be ten times as fast as Hoppy or Roy; he had to be because every bozo tried to demask the masked knight ... still, the Lone Ranger smiled, nothin rattled him.

Heigh ho Silver away ... there go the marbles of the forties ... the smell of decaying plush in the theatre, the thumping hearts of young boys and girls ... I wonder how many gals got hot for the masked man or wanted to feel up Tonto? But the loonies were good and clean so they hauled their asses through Steer City. Hoppy would never need penicillin to clean up clap. Hoppy was busy clearing the landscape of triggermen who made it unsafe for widows and bankers who wanted to run a decent town.

"Hurry, Kimisabe, Tombstone ..."

The smiling masked man wore a clean shirt. His duds shone ... clean bullet ... pure silver ... clean white hat ... and it was getting cold out on the desert, but their horses snuggled up to them. Warm decent flesh, clean desert air ... out there in space ... silver bullets sang across the horizon only they could see ... silver bullets ... in an endless shooting gallery ... silver bullets they believed would keep them from death as they rode determinedly on to Tombstone with ass-licking Tonto in the lead ... and they are out there in unmarked graves, all of them lying down together, hoss by jowl, escapees from the glue factory.

Survival

After the destruction of European Jewry, a separate Jewish state ceased to be a theoretical question. Intellectuals in the political and cultural mainstream had considered Zionism not only a Utopian concept, but reactionary – in that, instead of concentrating on forming a bond with other persecuted minorities, Zionists (whether left, right or centre) had taken the struggle outside their country to another territory.

To the death camp survivors, stateless people in refugee camps euphemistically called Displaced Persons, Zionism offered the only alternative; it meant a homeland where they could be rulers. Having battled the Nazis, the Jewish refugee had to fight the British in Palestine and at the same time keep the Palestinian Arabs at bay; victim had fallen upon another victim. A vicious war burst into the open, and for children like me at Lansdowne Public School, children informed that our race had been annihilated, the survivors were facing extinction again, this time at the hands of Arabs. It sent a murderous chill down our spines. We saw Palestinians not as a people fighting to hold on to their turf, but as an extension of Nazis bent on exterminating Jewish settlers, prepared to drive them into the sea... There was suddenly another game besides marbles, a game called survival.

The newspapers fed, they gorged on blood and violence. They gave the morning death scores. A bomb went off in a market place, so many Jews had died, columnists glitzed up the grisly details of the dead, the injured and cries for revenge. Another day, a bomb went off in an Arab market, and headlines screamed out the score. It depended whose side you were on; vile acts of brutality became a fixation for those actually fighting and for those in public relations or propaganda. I saw cruelty on every side, but I didn't want the Jews to lose. I knew one had to win or die; it appeared the Iraquis were not taking prisoners, that those who died fighting the Arabs had their bodies mutilated, genitals severed and shoved into their mouths, their ears cut off ... unspeakable acts, so we were told. Survival was the name, gore the game.

The Holocaust, and images of it, had molecular motions: we formed opposing groups in the schoolyard and although the school had a Jewish majority, there were pockets of resistence, non-Jews who sided with the Palestinians – not because they cared for the displaced Arabs, but because they had been taught to hate Jews.

As we kept up with the death scores in the headlines, our anger pitched high. We would be taunted by some gentile boy who had more gall than brains, and a good swift pair of running shoes. The insult rang in our ears: "Jew bagel, go back to Palestine." In his language, we were aliens because we sided with the remnants of the Holocaust. We weren't true natives. I became an extremist in an extreme situation; I couldn't be tepid in a bloody war; any sense of outrage had to be passionate: outrage ... the Red Baron stoned out of his skull on each kill ... a neutral stance or reasonable posture was repulsive. It gored me to hear voices call for moderation; it obviously hadn't worked in Europe, it wouldn't work in the Arab-Jewish conflict. I became an ultra-nationalist inflamed by images of Jewish corpses and the wounded mutilated by Arab guerillas. I envisioned doctors and nurses of the Jewish Red Cross who were massacred; gasoline drums exploded inside my skull. I envisioned a nurse raped, her breast slashed, a doctor his throat cut, a wounded soldier mutilated ... the burning ambulances and bodies sprawled on the roadside, photographed in exact detail ... all this suddenly vibrated my soul more than the fast draw of any gunslinger. There was an absolute range war going on that shot the flicks down the status pole. I shivered reading of the dead in combat.

I was an ultra Zionist, supporting the militants. They kept my speedometer going. Menachem Begin, who was on the run from the Tommies with a hefty price on his head, became my hero. Although respectable Laborites and other pinkos kept referring to him as a terrorist, I saw that the extremity of the situation, Jewish survival, needed a cut-throat engineer who could drive the British out of Palestine and booby-trap the pro-Hitler Arab boobs, make short shrift of them. In the paroxysm of violence, it was kill or be mutilated. Revenge echoed in my ears, blood for blood. When the gunsels of the Irgun iced a peaceful Arab village, *Dir Yasin*, I saw it as retribution for an iced Jewish Red Cross Convoy. My liberal playmates thought I was a frog from the pond of pestilence, an embarrassment to civilized Jewry. I told them their moderate methods would get them nowhere; the always polite British had applied terrorists tactics on an infinitely larger scale which we had yet to emulate. The British were out of the Holy Land because such impolite methods worked. Go Tell It To The Marines, I snorted like an animal who had just come into heat.

When the respectable wing of Zionism, the Establishment, sank an Irgun vessel out in Tel Aviv harbor and a number of Irgun lads died – killed by their racial comrades – I wept. A torrent of anger swept through my bile. It was the closest the Zionists had come to civil war, and the suction cups on my amphibious hands dearly wanted to crush the skulls of egghead Liberals; in my vitriolic condition, I began to imagine that the Zionist Establishment was sheepish. They were a bookish lot, *intellectuals*. How I hated that word; and the forced elocution of their speech and chauvinistic erudition bubbled on me like bad air. There was one lad who got my glue exuding; he had a tedious parliamentary habit: "I beg to differ..." I glowered as I came up with a slogan – Dynamite's The Stuff... Oh, I was a rare one in the schoolyard and cakeshops.

There were, however, limits even to the militants. The King David Hotel was totalled in '46 and Jews and British alike died in the explosion. I hung it out to dry but couldn't quite rationalize that: I argued that the British had deliberately disregarded the warning... Even then I knew it wasn't much of an argument. And when the boys almost strung up a Jewish lad they mistook as a Brit (Collins was his name and he started reciting Hebrew prayers and bubbled Yiddish phrases so that they had the rope off his neck quicker than you could say Holy Moly and had him back at his hotel lickety-split), I thought a few mistakes... who doesn't make them? Hadn't the Allies fired on their own troops when their logistics got glued up, and anyway, why hadn't Collins said his prayers quicker? For a moment, I almost thought it was Collins' fault.

So, I worry-warted around the fact they'd sent a plastic bomb to a British Blimp who had strung up a Jewish lad and instead got the man's brother in London. Another letter bomb and some kid had his hand blown away: it happens... you handle nitro, I said sagely, and some of the soup drops on the carpet... next time, the methods would be improved... so what else is new, huh...? A letter bomb goes astray.

My mind was keen as a switchblade... the British Lion was getting its tail wagged... and the news of the dead Jews handed over to Arab nutcutters... did that get any headlines? So, the Englishers rioted in London and went on a *jihad* crying for Jewish blood...! "What hypocrites," I shouted. "Go lick some Brit ass," I roared. My opponent quit begging to differ and threw in the towel. He called me a fascist, which I found odd, since the Maker Himself had shone His good clean light on my righteous cause, and now this pansy, this besmirched twerp, this lickspittle intellectual ...

Socialism had caught my fancy about this time, an inverted pyramid where the proletariat was no longer at the base of the pyramid but at the top ... prols ... farmers ... the idea seemed appetizing, and reading the Left Zionist brochures of the quasi-Marxist wing ... I concluded Israel needed its own brand of Socialism ... for Jews only ... fuck the rest of them ... Then, I remembered Mussolini had been a Socialist and that we needed a leader, a strong leader ... if only that boat had gotten through with those arms ... A simple putsch would do the trick ... and ZAP ... a stronger Israel ... not one ruled by intellectuals ... eggheads and other leeches that sucked on the backsides of the masses ... but an ingathering of Jews who had been forced to be tailors ... ragpickers ... bankers ... (I hated bankers and the bourgeoisie ... parasites ...) shoemakers ... chartered accountants ... but never farmers ... Yes, the pyramid had to be reversed ... the process of proletarianization accelerated ... a strong leader, a Jabotinsky, a Begin ...

I nurtured hatred and accepted its furry body. It was a dark creature, like a vole ... I hated overachivers and as far as I was concerned, Jews had always been overachievers in order to stay alive ... they got on the prayerwheel of social mobility and got past quota systems and therefore a horrid neurosis had wormed its way into the psychic properties of being human ... neurosis ... of the type that made Freud faint when contemplating the younger Jung ... a fear of having to be perfect ... to excel ... so that when I flunked in grade school, my gentile friends assumed my genetic strain was clouded ... somebody congratulated me for being the first dumb Jew he had set his eyes upon ... an underachiver ... he couldn't believe it ... I didn't palsy a marble ... fondle silver ... gamble ... but one taint remained: the kid *read* ... in fact, I not only read newspapers like they were going out of fashion, but books ... esoteric books on Beowulf ... King Arthur and the fucken Sword in the Lake with some loonie blond dame hunkering in the grass before the skin blade was stuck into her twilight by a knight in a rustproof suit ... my obsession with angelic light seemed awesome ...

But the news ate me up. Some nutbar – by the unprounceable name of Fawzi el Kazi – had taken a shine to blowing up Jewish market places. He was so good at it that I began to hate him; he was an overachiever; the boys couldn't keep up with his score. Nobody could ice him quick enough. The bomber ruined my appetite. I remember leaning over an overgenerous portion of succulent corn-beef, my epiglotis expanding and contracting, there it was in the prints, his latest hit ... the fucker ... the meat, piping hot with a plate of dills with an amazing mixture of spice, *secret* spice ... (it had been in the family for decades –) and my taste buds died ... My head exploded: somebody blow that shitface Fawzi away ... It turned out that Fawzi not only got away with it, but the fellow was a gynocologist!

But my best vole was for the Grand Mufti of Jerusalem, who had been decorated by Hitler, and he had promised the Exterminator his loyalty in fighting the British and, of course, the Jews. I associated all Palestinians with the Mufti ... instantly every Arab became a Nazi ... and my militancy transformed me into a hater: Arab armies were sweeping into Palestine ... they were serious about pushing the Jews into the sea ...

Rumors were abound ... Zionist sympathizers buying shotguns in the big department stores and these were bundled away to the front ... somehow, I couldn't see anybody buying shotguns, but it was a wonderful myth ... what was real, however, was the build-up of the Zionist army by purchasing WW 2 weapons from Czechoslovakia and the armament of words ... the rallies and the support they received from Christians who were Zionists ...

I recall a parade that began one Saturday in the schoolyard: the marching ranks and captains ... placards ... and out of the yard onto Bathurst Street to College, and then East along College Street ... thousands joined the parade as volunteer canvassers stopped cars for donations ... the parade ending up at Maple Leaf Gardens ... swarming into the entrances and packing the building ... and emblazoned across the stage, a banner fluttered: GIVE US THE TOOLS AND WE'LL FINISH THE JOB ...

This was a mass rally to get arms for the Jewish State. Thousands waited for the ceremony to begin, supporting the one cause that thrummed in every heart: Survival. There were wardheelers, labor leaders, senators, teachers, tycoons ... and each speaker walked directly to the podium: some spoke coolly, others used a trim phrase or a manicured tongue ... but there were those who spat out fire and brimstone ... who thumped a fist on the podium, raged, emoted some gut-mad phrase and rolled their sleeves up and like a spring bull, raged: Give us the tools and we'll finish the job, and thousands stood and roared ... and one speaker intimated that Israel needed arms even if the Devil himself pushed them in their direction ... "A bullet has no smell." Everybody on the platform buried their differences; nobody said that Stalin, who had recognized the Israelis' was a Georgian Rat who'd got goosed by his buddy Hitler ... "Give us the tools," shouted the audience.

The Egyptians were using German scientists ... rocket research, and rockets were going to be aimed against the state of Israel ... I envisioned little brown savages invading, slitting throats ... they were from the Sudan, and then by an act of God, a truce was agreed upon; it gave the Israelis time to whip the Czeck hardware into shape, an airforce ... and tanks ... and somebody had sold the Arabs arms so defective they blew up in their faces ... the armies that poured into Palestine had no central command ... but it was to the most machined fighters in the area – the British-trained Jordanian army – that the bedraggled Jewish fighters surrendered Jerusalem to, and I recall seeing a blown-up photograph of the surrender: rabbinical students escorted by rabbis who turned over their arms to solemn troops in kahki uniforms ... the land had been gained but the holy city had been lost ...

Crunchdale sneered at us. Chick said little. It is hard to know what side they would have chosen. It wasn't their war. It never is. Political climates come and go, and sometimes what emerges is a desert where greeny passion thrives, and feet storm on the road.

City Wild Life: Ants, Bugs, Bread Mould, or the Heat of '48

The heat that followed me around the city would have roasted a brigade of fire ants if I'd only basted their scent trails with butter. A shy boy, I had a tendency to stare at my feet, and Chick's every effort to arrest my blooming spinal curvature failed. My shyness, although it led to sloped shoulders, nevertheless proved compensatory. I discovered a world that struggled under my feet: the casualties of a summer scorcher whose humidity licked my face and arms. Plainly, the heat wave's personality disorder drove the congregants of a black and red ant church mad. They rushed from the sidewalk cracks shaking a deadly dew before collapsing into endless mounds of private funeral pyres: a lunatic lad passed a magnifying glass and incinerated the lot, the vicious rays of the sun pouring through the lens. The fiendish punk laughed while the ants burst into flames in miniaturized sequences: a puff ... smoke ... and an orange-magenta flamboyance, or glow ... a few survivors of the cosmic jokester fled along the curb or the fringes of a lawn. The mass ant roast provided a welcome, although sick, relief for me ... a cheap flick, a free movie. Those images of proletarian miniscule deaths held the attention of other tourists and malcontents whose parents couldn't afford to send them out of the city to a rustic landscape – to see the real thing, a cow ... a moose ... anything but a city ant.

I made a bet with myself: those ant swarms that were still alive were praying for a cold rain to wash them back to the realm of the living. The ants expired in the millions ... If I closed my eyes and concentrated on a speck of a flame it grew in length and I heard the song of that jet burner; and if I kept my concentration intact, I detected bubble glue exuding from nowhere, from a tiny sleeve in the darkness and that spittle moved as molasses would, probed by a tongue of heat. The gluey trail lead to the land of steak tartare, a meaty paradise alongside an oasis of blood; to add further to this grotesque manifestation, another spectre crossed my field of vision, giving an edge to the grim reality: a winged ant invasion from some inner space; they didn't arrive out of the air above me, but at my feet, swooping down on the pagans and they tore them to pieces for a soup base; having sated themselves silly with meat and drink, they fled like wolves on the wings of an obscene prayer.

As I mentioned, the unfolding hymenopterous homicide kept me from going mad in the heat. Summer camp resided somewhere in my brain, distant, and not nearly as delicious as those obtainable sights. I could dream about crystalline waters gurgling under the surface of a very blue lake, and yet it wasn't the stuff that the brain found tactile, it wasn't city wild life beckoning for your complete attention, a jungle under the fine white grains of sand between the cracks of the boiling sidewalk ... tigers in the guise of ants, winged or unwinged ... munching, bleeding, a death agony under the blade of one lonely finger ... a green tongue of grass ... a palm tree of a dandelion with a corpse stretched at its base ... Who cared about a mottled cow? Here, there were flying predators lunging at the roof of an ant struggling to ward off the deranged demon ...

Supposing the Engineer who built the whole system was a flying ant? Why should the Boss build his image in a man when there were other exciting options open ... more intricate biologic systems and compound visions; imagine the Creator in the form of a June bug? My reverence for them came about when I accidently stepped on one and the creature blithely walked away from under my feet; or at least, he walked away to die on his own turf, exploding on the lawn from injuries sustained, and a white glue leaked from under that wicked carapace as though the bug had fouled its own house, protesting my accidental assassination. It leaped once or twice to make its lewd point before perishing.

The summer bullies made the scene during that same scorcher, jiving under the haze, boogeying along, clattering their wings, and time and again they struggled to take flight only to splatter the roads, or any available landing field. They were guests who crashed your house, dived into your supper, struck your window pane leaving a line of disgusting glue and other noxious fluids; the bullies exploded on impact (I swear it made the sound of a bursting roach pregnancy). They fouled the windows, and even the windows of the mind wouldn't open to such a frightful sight. I turned away from the guts of each damaged lichee nut of a june bug; they froze on the glass, leaving their obscenities as instant monuments to a joyless viewer. It seemed that they wanted to die, for they waited as if in ambush, to be stepped upon; and it appeared evident that this was their collective plan: self destruction. They chose the absolute microsecond to surrender their life to a pedestrian's shoe leather, bursting under foot like a grape in heat ...

I watched for any possible trap. I looked to my left and right, measuring every step, but it proved futile. They shouted up at me: Step on me. Step on me, and it would have been sadistic not to honor their wishes. And so they died, a vibrating death song under their wings.

I kept my eyes on ambush; my lights searched for a brown dancer jiving on the sidewalk, singing some dirty song, and I kept my mouth shut: I was sure june bugs had the horrid habit of zipping at your face. The thought of a june bug flying into my mouth was enough to send a yellow stream down my pant leg. It made me vigilant; my vigilance seemed mechanical, like every step I made on the road. It was a combat alert situation, mouth closed, eyes riveted to the ground, and hands ready to slap a winged excrementious bastard away. I kept my gates closed. The bugs smelled fear and were turned on by human sweat which meant I constantly ran into the house and scrubbed the sweat off with soap and very cold water. I gave myself the shakes. Strangely, no june bug dashed at me. Their sudden visitations were only at my feet, a sick song being the first indication that the bullies were there.

The demented swarms of brown shelled protein carpeted the sidewalks, crept into cracks along the sides of buildings, and sometimes they cleverly got into an open sock hanging on a line, or crept into anything open; a boiling pot on the stove, anywhere they could lie down and join their ancestors. This foulest of manna vibrated through the air with songs of the stagnant heart. That was it, perhaps: I understood intuitively that they were foul manna, the evening droppings of the presence of evil, evil being the stagnant heart. The most delicious sight, therefore, was that of a robin or other under-sized chicken tearing open the bugs. I carefully noted the symbiotic relationship between bird and bug. It was a marriage made in hyper-heaven ... an intense union ...

Given this obsession with the brown dancers of the air, penicillin became a preoccupation as well. It conjured images, even to this day, of a blue accidental mould on bread, pampered, allowed to reach its deepest mould, ripened, and synthetized until it became a killer mould trapping infection, eating infection raw.

And now the mould, the champagne of moulds, attacked clap and other venereal diseases of the body and soul; the magic mould turned all infection into nothing more harmful than a bad cold. Mould meant you didn't need to have your water works cleaned out with a hot needle. I knew it was growing on some old rye bread in the cupboard. I let the mould grow in several places on wet bread, and had specimens for an experiment I carried out in my mind, an experiment which shadowed Frankenstein who groomed a brain for his monstrous creation, cultivating his brain harvest under glass, fed on fluids and lightning. I let my mould grow as affordable brains in jars, brains that would absorb all infection of the spirit, brains that would stare unflinchingly into the eye of the june bug.

"And I Thought You Were Selling Knowledge"

The encyclopedia salesman squared-off like the books he held up to the householder. Between the pages of the book, a condom magically appeared before the customer's astonished peepers. The man gazed down at the champagne of rubber, *Ramses* – and it stood out among other samples the knowledgeman pushed in the neighborhood. By the shine in the man's eyes, the salesman knew his product spoke louder than verbal expositions. The householder's eyes warmed to the handsomely packaged rubber with its logo that suggested not only nobility but a nomad, a roving soul out on a sand dune ... stirring a twinge of class consciousness, as it suggested the affordable for the masses and the "safe" pleasures of a prince amongst common fornicators. All other rubberware suggested defects; they weren't as lead-proof as the champagne item. This notion was in the consumer's subconscious long before the salesman darkened the householder's door; the man didn't need his sales pitch ... "I'm selling a hundred percent prevention and I'm not talking ninety nine percent, no sir ... one hundred percent ... more doctors recommend ..."

Still, the salesman caught a line of doubt in his customer's facial armor. Like it or not, price remained the issue. This householder had the expression of an alley cat, a real scrapper. The salesman continued, "And you don't get any dose with these rubbers, let me tell you ... they're the best." The householder's eyes had now shifted to a strangely packaged rubber with a darker logo depicting a rutting reptile. He made out the figure of an alligator. Suddenly, in an action which surprised him, he let his finger tips graze the surface of the product. "What is this?" the man said, quickly drawing back his fingers as though he had made contact with a diseased organ. "Holy Moly, this rubber's got the pox ... shit your rubber has got some kind of leprosy." The salesman chuckled, the hook was set, the champagne rubber piece had been a decoy.

"Mister," the salesman replied with triumphal emphasis in his shrill voice. "You are looking at the best, the tabu of rubber ... the secret weapon that does the work for you, and I have, yes I have,

TESTIMONIALS that can't say enough for this rubber, and you know this stuff is so hot that they don't sell it in the drugstores cause it is still in its experimental stage and I have it, a limited run, and it makes the Ramses look like a street bum ... a cheap Ford to a Rolls Royce of absolutely perfect, hand crafted, not machined for mass production ... and ..."

"What is the bumps for ... that don't make sense ... and the double header on the tip looks like the rubber has got a bad boil ... like some kind of blister with a lot of water in it if you understand my meaning."

The salesman had a sculptured imperial smile on his lips. "The alligator texture drives the ladies wild ... Now, I don't have to tell an intelligent man like you why it drives them crazy with desire and do I have to tell you that the tip as you call it ... the blister as you vulgarly put it ... massages the ..."

"You don't mean it tickles them," interjected the householder, who suddenly had the feeling the salesman had put a dunce cap on his crown. The householder laughed, and by this he hoped his self-contempt would neutralize his diminished stature before such an aristocrat among salesmen ... "And all the time I thought you was selling Knowledge ... and here you are selling ticklers." The salesman laughed. He knew the man's predicament, but the laughter had a hollow sound. The householder again ran his fingers across the alligatorial skin and shook his head in disbelief. He viewed the product as a perversion, yet desirable.

"It's called the French tickler," the salesman said, seeking the high moral ground through precision. "The rubber is called *Gator Lover*, and it's manufactured by a small concern in the States ... as I said it is experimental ... and the company don't want any publicity ... but let me assure you ... it's safe ... reliable ... you could wear it on your feet and climb Mount Vesuvius ... the rubber simply hasn't got an elastic limit ... you need dynamite to break this material ... and ..."

The salesman pressed closer to the man's face. He whispered aloud ... "You can use it over and over again ... wash it down and it's good as new ..."

"I don't believe it," the householder replied, and brushed his fingers across the rubber like one who read braille.

"You see Sir (he emphasized Sir), the girls' gaggle at your powers ... it's the chemicals in the rubber ... does something to the hormonal flow ... (the man pouted out FLOW). I tell you Sir, there's power steering in this bit of rubber ..."

The householder expectorated, his mind alive with images of carnal alchemy ... power ... thrusts ... gyrations ...

"And I mean sir, it's the best ... not just any rubber, but the supernatural of rubbers itself ... the libido in magic rubber ... the Top Hat among poontang Ticklers."

There was nervous dew on the Knowledgeman's brow. Suddenly, the salesman sensed he had gone too far; if he didn't give the fellow back his small intellectual crown, he would plainly lose a sale; the customer needed reinforcement the way a child needs special attention at the very beginning of life's travail. Each individual has his or her special space capsule; even a worm has its time machine, so everything has to be seen in context ... the householder had his text and it had to be read before he could be conned.

The salesman was clearly pushing a shameful substance. Not many clowns marched into a drugstore and asked for rubber, certainly not if there was a lady pharmacist behind the counter. Even if the rubber dwelt in a bubblegum machine, it existed in full view and the people would sneer and think to themselves, there goes a sex maniac ... a mindless unlicensed pump man ... for what harried all such men was shame. Understand a man's source of shame and you've got him by the short hairs (a man with no shame is a potential power steering fascist). How could a man ashamed of his little watering can ask for Gator Lover ... that would be like asking for smack ... snow ... from your local zonked-out smiling druggist ... Gator Lover meant the wild insane rubber ... the tickler that left a transparent foam of ectasy on a woman's lips like the foam from a hummingbird's wings as it left the calyx of a flower ...

"So this is the French tickler," the householder said again, loudly, as he resisted the urge to fondle the condom. "It sure does look scary ... I mean them bumps ... Hell, it could cause bleeding to both parties ... if you fathom my meaning ... and the bubble massager ... Now, that is interesting."

The salesman, glowing from the nervousness which conjoined them, was wise enough to keep silent, to let the householder shed his own shame. The salesman felt only a tick of guilt, like a true believer selling a crucifix to a cannibal. "Prevention" then bubbled off the salesman's lips with the gravity of morality ... God ... Moses ... and he spoke of prophylaxis with a solemnity worthy of the topic of trepanning ... pull the skull flap back.

"Alright," the householder suddenly blurted, wanting to buy ... but how ...?

"I'll buy your fuckin lettuce ... alright ... How much?"

The householder notes the manicured lawn on the salesman's head, close-cropped, a college kid, a future oral surgeon.

"So, I'll buy your FUCKEN rubber alright." He passed the

salesman a finsky (five dollars on the hoof) and a few coins were plunked in the palm of the purchaser.

"Jeez, I'm not buying the moon. How much can a tickle in life cost?"

"I'm selling a clean product, mister..."

"That's funny," the householder sneered. "I thought you were selling knowledge ... Yeah, put it in your ear punk ..." Still, the man needs his miracle rubber, and he is no match for the sheepish egghead who backs away from the door as a voice passes between them like a razor blade, shaving the tension.

"Who's that, Harry ... tell the man to go away ... we don't need anything ... Harry ... are you listening?"

"Alright, Suzzie, hold on to your button ... it's a college kid selling Books of Knowledge."

"We don't need to know nothing, Harry."

Harry turns to the salesman, fire shining in his lights. "Buzz off. You hear that flyface! Buzz off."

Suddenly the giantess bobs into the doorway. She has cantaloupes for mammaries but seems to have only one eye in the center of her forehead. She is several ax handles across the back and her hands are immense. She could be in drag because the blond piece on her head appears to be as loose as her lips, which are now crossed by a lascivious, malevolent smile.

"Don't talk to the boy like that. Say you're sorry. What's your name cutie?"

The salesman edges out into the street. "No name," he says. "Just nobody."

"There was nobody at the door," she cries, and cackles. "What were you saying, Harry, since nobody was here?"

"Nothing *Honeycup*, my little Suzzie."

The door slams shut. The salesman works up the bubble of an image: in the darkness of the bedroom, the Gator will fit like a rigid stamen into a soft calyx, the interior of a meat eating orchid.

Experiments in Mood Food

I placed a salamander in an empty Planter's Peanut wrapper where it died in the salt, but not before changing into several rubbery suits of color. The fiendish cellophane condom let me study the various hues the animal suffered; I had clear images of the creature struggling to stay alive as salt absorbed its very life. It changed from a citrinous green to a deeper viridescence. In protracted demise, it sent out a black thread of tongue, pleading for its life and when that plea failed, the salamander's outfit became a green funeral suit. The thready tongue quivered; it looked ever so cute in the death chamber with its black pin hole of a mouth ...

The poor lizard spasmed and then lay perfectly still, dying just as Eddy had croaked in the gas chamber. Eddy probably turned as green as the salamander, though he took a different kind of salt. I wonder what bad air went into my mind as I conducted this sickly experiment? I saw how the lizard hugged life, how it stroked the walls of the wrapper with its wee webbed hands, all the while its tongue, the most tactile of its organs, touched the interior of that transparent tomb but not my heart. A vacuous act. I now forget why I conducted the experiment: perhaps to match up colors and test the range of the chimeral captive and observe its actual chromatic vocabulary? Sounds good. I should have cried, felt remorse, shock, and not just thin surprise. Eddy had deserved it; the salamander had harmed no one except a few mosquitos. That sounds good, too: we're caught, it seems, between two extremes – the sentimental and the sadistic. Anyway, I had found the sexy lizard in the grass. The soft lime yellow attire betrayed its presence against a darker carpet. A milisecond later and the animal might have turned the correct color and I surely would have missed it. Camouflage. Perhaps camouflage is the secret to survival and the happy life. Whatever, I held up the rubbery body, watching it yearn for the tincture of sky blue. The empty Planter's Peanut wrapper was intended as a temporary holding cell (death cells usually are, in every revolution) and I had no inkling as to what salt would do to my salamander. Murder wasn't in my heart. I didn't conduct a thousand poor lizards to their deaths. I was no degenerate doctor waving his victims to their deaths with a white glove. I was more stupid than cruel. That sounds good, too, for there is a molecule of the murderer in every one of us. How does it all begin? Every killer, even Eddy, was an infant once and somehow an evil seed progressed. The execution of the salamander, intentional or not, indicated a snag in a child's psychic growth, and that opens another condom of worms: is the killer born or made?

You start somewhere ... with a bullfrog, dissecting the straddler, who gorges on flies, snapping those raisins of the sun. The bullfrog's dismembered legs, wired to a battery's terminals, wag and seem to applaud the knife. Does the body tremble under the knife as in love? Is this mystery always only a stone's throw away. I bounced a rock off a bullfrog's head. I don't know why I did it. The straddler leaned into the stream just before going over the falls, and then it gladdened me that no evidence of my foul deed lay about with its one good eye staring at me. The amphibian ended in a whirlpool, dragged under forever, but the green victim swims in my brain, his webbed hands reaching out to me. My brain is a cellophane condomn containing flying fish and sea urchins, salamanders and the sarcophagi of a thousand other serendipitous creatures, all salted away, the mood food of melancholy and meditation. That sounds good, too.

Pike the Milkman

The strap resembled a leather snake. It hung by the side of the door in Mr. Pike's office. Pike, our principal, seldom strapped a student but just in case some spirochette of a student should infect the scholastic body, the leather beast provided ample warning: the snake had its place in the system. Sometimes it sang.

Pike stared at me with the lights of a Dalai Lama, the hurt expression of someone who, moments ago, had foolishly stepped on the household kitten and now had to witness the mother cat licking a dead child. What buried moments of enraged assault did he carry in his heart? What inexplicable explosion of anger against a child had left him with these kind, hurt eyes. His brown peepers were set deeply in the sockets: he seemed like one who had heard the angels of conscience at his elbow. His weakness was the swollen aphorism. He swabbed the lens of his imagination and let an aphorism grow.

The Lord does not smile kindly on those boys who shirk their earthly work. They are like an indolent lizard who thinks only of sunning its belly in the glory of our Savior.

Echoes of aphorism cling to my memory: *go the way of the lamb and have the heart of the lion* falls gently into the darkness. Surrounded by vases of freshly cut lilies (at least I think they were lilies –) the old man mumbled on about the loaf of honest industry and the sweat of one's brow, for a good laborer is worthy of his hire though he must eat a peck of dirt before he dies ... and on and on until I swore the lilies opened their pure mouths and dumped golden pollen on Pike's lap. He had duck yolk orange pollen on the sleeves of his Harris Tweed jacket and some holy dust glowed from his pin-striped charcoal-grey trousers. Obviously, he fondled blooms as well as the Holy Book. A refulgent tear glistened in the corner of his eye. No matter the provocation, he tried to resist the snake, instead offering the student a twig from his floral collection. It amazed me when, at the last moment, he flung the snake aside as though it were a disease, and in lieu of a rejected orchid, offered an aphorism about pits, burning sulphur and devils who stung the flesh of idlers who infected others, but there seemed time to avoid the abyss if only the shoulder was put to the wheel, to the grindstone ... a suggestion that puzzled me: a shoulder bone being ground down on a wheel. Pike stroked a long pencil. Occasionally, he stabbed the large ink blotter on his desk. The desk was meticulous. Nothing appeared out of place. Pencils neatly sharpened lay in a row; the tips of his fountain pens were clean; they shone in the afternoon sunlight. Pike glowed like the tips of his fountain pens.

I see him: he's leaning back in his armchair, staring directly at me, holding me in his hurt gaze. The light pours in from the window facing the schoolyard. I see the hairline receding, the hair combed stiffly back, and by its texture and gloss, I know he has cultivated that plot of hair as carefully as an aphorism. The receding hairline denotes the tidal line in his affairs, the hint of mortality and the discard pile for Pike (he was then a year away from retirement). His white, white teeth clash with his purplish lips, and yet they complement his oyster white hair. His black bowtie blends in perfectly with his pasturized white shirt; nothing is out of place, and everything seems to have the air of well-distributed weight, so that his suspenders suggest strength. There is no ash tray in his office. He never smokes, nor is there ever a trace of alcohol on his breath. Pike never says *damn*.

He presses a pamphlet into my hands, issued to parents to impress upon them the need of a balanced diet. Pike draws my attention to wholewheat bread ... fish ... eggs ... vegetables ... and there are symbols beside each drawing giving the mineral properties of each item ... valences of health ... togetherness ... and a small child peeps out from the corner of the page depicting the nuclear family ...

I'm made aware of iron ... magnesium ... good fibre ...

"What did you eat this morning, son?" I'm lost for an answer. How can I tell him I ate porridge, that I detest spinnach, that porridge reminds me of glue? I am sure Christ wouldn't eat the stuff, or multiply it. Pike suddenly breaks into ectoplasmic brilliance: No sugars, and no smoking. "Love milk," he cries. He jabs his finger (so manicured that I assume it has been trimmed by elves) at a mottled cow on the nutrition sheet. Milk, milk, milk, milk, he chants like a maniac. I back away from his desk. "Beware of the limbless one," he hisses as I slip out of his office. "Son, there are bad apples out there. There are tubes in the cosmos." And then he stood up, that wounded, distressed look in his eyes and he grabbed the strap from the wall and made it sing across the desk, the crack of live snake across solid oak, and he cried, "For he on milk and honeydew hath fed ... weave a circle round him thrice."

Miss Blossoms

Miss Blossoms stroked a tuning fork across my knuckles for having the temerity to say *damn. Doe Ray me Fah So La Te Doe ... ohhh.*

Damn, I had said, disappointed that I hadn't plucked the heights. That's when she whipped out her tuning fork and gave me a low blow.

Doe oooooooh, she screamed, her bra shifting, clapping my knuckles fiercely. They bled. She was a stick, her legs a little thicker than broomsticks, and her whole frame, or however you might describe the lean-to shed of meat she displayed publicly, heaved with her concerns for my singing the scales aloud. My voice gagged her. There was an element of insult in the way I blew out the sound. It grated on her nerves, puffed out her arms, and her neck suddenly turned red as a beet or other bleeding vegetable matter. She warmed up her still of hidden hatred and irritated her asthma. She gagged, coughed, wheezed, and the wheezing sent a chill down to my liver. *Eeeeeeeeeeee* and *Eeeeeee*, she gasped. *Eeeeee*, she spat, gurgled, spattered, suffering from the furies below her neckline. *Eeeee*, the sputum burst in her throat, her eyes rolled in rhythm with her attacks. Was she going to croak? And then, the rasping voice, a voice within a voice, spectral, and yet earthy, rose from the pits of her stomach and rattled her chest-lining. It took on more sputum and infections, clattering around in mid-chest above her withered breasts, her prunes that took on a life of their own, a life denied. She hated me because she was no singer herself. She was a screamer, tone deaf to joy. She knew joy existed but had never known it. So she ran up and down the scales, cracking tuning forks across the knuckles of little children, as if the knuckle could be the source of musicality, as if the knuckle could carry a tune. I am convinced that when she fell out from the birth cavity and hung like a phone cord with a babe at the other end, there wasn't a child there but an old woman. She never had a youth.

I hated her. I hated music and associated musical notation with blood and pain. She beat my knuckles until they bled. I realized I could never make the angels weep with the voice the Maker had given me: one sound seemed the same as another, and a soprano quaver in my voice was just a sonic chore. She couldn't take the sound, I couldn't take the pain, especially on the mid-knuckle when the bleeding wouldn't stop and took weeks to heal; there seemed to be no coagulation there.

She turned her bony shoulders and whipped out some fiendish inhalator and blew a perfumed blast down her gullet ... *Eeeeeeee*, she squeeled ... *Eeeeee*. The crap in her epiglotal section dissolved and a jet of air sucked through her wind pipe, lifting her withered tits up and down. Miss Blossoms convinced me that her brown dried face was older than any bandaged stiff in a cool crypt.

Eeeeee. I prayed she would die. She sucked in the thin atmosphere of the inhalator; it filled the pouches of her cheeks, and then her eyes rolled, suggesting clearance not only of her bronchial tubes but the brain passages as well. A normal coloration that we associate with the living came back to her complexion. The flesh took on a pink and a white flush.

"Now children," she said, her voice ringing. "Please pay attention, your ears, please."

Smirking rather than smiling, she raised a tuning fork above her head like some missionary carrying a small silver cross into the darkness of iniquity and brought the instrument down on the edge of her desk, making it ring until the vibrations shook the roots in our gums. The supernatural heart of baby Jesus, a disembodied sound, seized the class like a cry for help: what terrible fate, I wondered, had befallen the baby Jesus?

Doe ray me fah so lahtee doe oooooo, her voice riding the sound waves. An electrical field took possession of her. There was one quick hacking cough. She spat a spot of blood on a lace handkerchief. I had witnessed the blood shining on her magnesium-white lips. She wanted to sing, wanted to sing more than anything. I should have loved her, but I hated her. It was all a cruel joke. She'd been born at the end of her blooming and yet was called Miss Blossoms. It was blood that blossomed on her thin lips. The tubes of the cosmos were sucking her frail body into a silent lung sac, along with her damned tuning fork of a lightning rod. A scream oozes out of those mnemonic bones.

Miss Pettybones

She had a hugely magnificent dread of Satan's Sup, alcohol. She made sly, oblique allusions to animal urges by which she meant sex. The term *sex* never surfaced. Animal urges (even heat sufficed) lost their meaning: they seemed to include any pleasures experienced by the living on the planet, which took in eating or listening to raucous sounds on the radio; corruption included anything that gave any pleasure to conductor or conduit – anything that opened the libido in the brain, anything that meant touching, anything that involved the hands. Heaven only knows what she thought of self-abuse, or onanism. She was not old but she had a septuagenarian heart, and even though no eye is more severe and unforgiving than the child's, I think I am right. She saw hair in the palm of all emotion.

Kissing was tabu. Lips were decorative, and I discovered a phobia she had by pure chance. *Damn*, I had said, and you'd have thought I'd vomited into her speckled ear. "Oh!" she gasped, falling back in her chair, turning a pale salmon pink, as though the word *damn* aroused a dark seed in her body, inflamed an organ long out of use. "Never, never, EVER say DAMN." She squealed. DAMN aloud to the class. Saying it gave her perverse pleasure. I had just witnessed my very first audio flasher. After she'd exposed her DAMN to the classroom, and when the high point of DAMN reached the ceiling, her breathing suddenly appeared erratic. I think it was my first sexual experience ... unique in that there was no penetration except sound itself. DAMN DAMN I repeated softly, perplexed, and maybe she climaxed secretly, one of those quiet jobs. Her brown eyes rolled in the cerebral jelly. Somehow the damn served as an after-audio – as a star, when it explodes, leaves an impression of its demise, or an *afterimage* which lasts for centuries, a ring of cosmic dust trapped in time. The resonance of damn. "Oh, child," she squeaked again, "never EVER use DAMN. A dam is a wall holding back or containing a body of water."

I agreed to polite silence but she persisted. She became possessed. An echo aroused the sublime trigger to her darkest pleasures, and now that I reflect on the matter, perhaps she was the type who – in slightly different times – would pay a young male to assault her sensibilities. Bliss her out with sonic profanities. Her eyes bloomed when I repeated BODY OF WATER ...

Later, I uttered ass, the little beast who carried infant Jesus into Jerusalem and she blinked in disbelief. *Uuuu* she hissed. *Uuuuu*. An animal sound a ferret might have released in the woods. She puckered her lips. "*Asssss,*" she hissed. She blinked. "Never EVER say that again. Naughty." I apologised for the baby Jesus, but the laughter in the class would have driven Ming the Merciless off a sand dune on Planet Mongo. Pettybones turned a deeper hue of salmon pink, embarrassed for both of us. I believe she liked me and only wanted to protect me, not only from a sound but its harsher associations. Clearly, my young soul had been released into a corrupted world. An amputee (like Miss Plover), she raised her bad arm, which seemed to have been cleaved off neatly below the elbow, when she was full of righteousness and anger. The stump vibrated. Sometimes when tenderness and temerity had taken her, she concealed the flesh with an old sock, and covered, the offending stump ceased to mesmerize us. Still, the stump clung to her like a dangling participle, and she often talked with relish and over-cooked horror of how a dangling participle could ruin our young lives. But some days the angle of the dangle seemed to equal the heat of the meat. On those days, she flashed her stump in the buff. On those days, secret urges seemed to get the best of her. Did she suffer from the ghost limb effect? She jabbed the stump at us if we laughed when we shouldn't have, or when she slipped us a quickie line or two from the Old Testament. She tried to flash some Jesus at us too, refusing to recognize that most of her kids were Jewish. But she beat out the message, thumping her stump on the table when she read from the Apostles ...

"Now, children," she said calmly, "next week we'll talk about John." She selected someone to pass out another Evangelical pamphlet. She gripped the pamphlets and punched them with her well-socked stump. "Here is the word of Salvation," she said. "John, next week," and she smiled, listening to sonic pleasures beyond our small ears.

But to this day, over and over I say it: *damn damn* and somewhere glow worms dance in the ice and the sock is taken off the stump, and the stump wags in the buff, sutured, alone.

Glue, the Serpent, and Lunch

Possibly – the bullfrog having fallen asleep – is a victim of the bucolic atmosphere lingering below his soft green crown. It has lulled him into a complacency, so that the straddler is vulnerable to deadly elements. The stillness of the landscape is consistent with another sunny afternoon. Victor, let's call him Victor, feels like dreaming about a fat summer fly lured from a humming cosmos down to the Earth. A ripened black manna of hymenopterous jiving fly, pure sky chicken to a bullfrog. Anyway, that hot manna is the straddler's ethnic food. Now, how do I know that Victor is not Victoria? Well, because Victor isn't weighed down with eggs in his tummy, and his yawn isn't as melodious, as lyrical or as sveltic as Victoria's reverberating croak. There's too much belch in his tight yawn. Victor is sleeping a little away from the margins of the lake, the day's heat having penetrated his rubbery diving suit, the amino acids have percolated and are working through the fatty tissue. In short, Victor is feeling warm all over.

An itch comes upon him, the kind of animal heat that affects straddlers. On the computer screen of his mind, cerebral dots form a female bullfrog with large open egg sacs on her back. Victor has to get off on those foetal froglins closed inside their pupas or dermal incubators, but alas, it's only the flow of the brain's impulses ... not coporeal, like the real meat, when his copulative urges wet the exposed areas of his lady's back ...

Victor feels a tightening in his tight apparel (his outfit tends to become flabby, depending on the hibernation cycle) and then there is a craving to fold up in a foetal position and play the frogling bursting out of confinement, emerging into full froginess. The rational hemisphere in Victor's brain informs him that the best thing next to prison break, or the real act of coition, is making it with some sky chicken or roof meat, as he calls it. His tongue darts out. An imaginary fly alights on the tongue and the roof chicken is glued to that bridge, Oblivion. *Ummm*, murmurs Victor, and the murmur aches in his soul. Zap, the chicken disappears in his volatile mouth, which is always motoring. Now, does a bullfrog lick his lips? All the world is an open kitchen, as some Amphibious Shakespeare would have put it. Victor loves his chicken because the next day may be raining not chicken but water; he needs his meat more than cosmic lachrymose. He throws his webbed hands and feet back and oozes into a deeper slumberous motel. He stretches his webbed hands as if playing soft ball with a fly. The stretch relieves the pressure on his umpteen glands and prevents his birthday suit from becoming too greasy.

Now, if Victor is hungry for skychicken, then some wandering land eel is slumming for a hot piece of frog flesh. The tube being apodal has to make it through life on his belly (or her belly) by expanding and contracting the skin, and if the poor tube rubs too much of his rubber he'll need a retreading job, but that's another story. As for the tube, I'll call him Herschel. He loves an easy mark on Nature's vast fast food floor, one that won't fight back, an easy rape, a slam-bam-thank-you-mam lunch, because where there's one straddler there's always another dummy around: straddlers are dreamy and slow. Victor is dreaming himself off (there's no end to onanism) and doesn't know the limbless Nemesis is lingering about, but Emma does – and who is Emma? That's my name for Victor's girl friend, the one he keeps on the back burner when he isn't marsh hopping with Marsha. Now Emma has the smarts which Victor doesn't, and she is hiding behind some ferns. Emma emits a signal that only another frog can hear. In fact, Herschel doesn't have ear canals, no audio-tentacles, nothing. So Victor should have the advantage in *An Early Warning System Against Tubal Surprises*. An E.W.S. A.T.S. Emma tries. A sonic wave. Another. Seconds to go. Tube is turning around a casual corner. Tube is grinning. Meat on the beach. And they say there's no serpent god. What snake shit! *Ummm*, a live palpitating hunk of frog.

If she could leap on his stomach and do a webbed tap dance she would. But it's useless, Victor is in limbo swamp world on a brain surd. She could rub her back on his wide face and it wouldn't help. Victor is in webbed wonderworld of hot sky chicken, eggs egging to be fertilized, an Ego straddler's star city ...

The tube is turning around the bend of bullrushes.

"I can't believe it," says the tube, expelling bad air. "The Lord hath delivered unto me a fat cow, blessed be the Lord..."

He can't believe his luck and hasn't had a good meal since he knocked off a field mouse, one with tits, eleven months pregnant, full of the sweetbreads of rodental ligature. "Thank ye, Lord ... oh what a sumptious meal blessed by thy rays."

Herschel is beside himself. He can't go home to Eden but what the hell, such is the fruit of the tree. He is hot and heavy, his tummy groaning for bulk food. He'll try the green clown.

Now, a bit about Herschel's memory bank. He is an orphan, and a bitter one at that. His mother died of the heart break that snakes often get; Herschel's dad was offed by a snow owl. Having lost his eelish folks, he had to fend for himself. In short, a mud-wise snake. But he's one, alas, suffering from convoluted hysteria. Since the death of his parents, the hands of Ra armed his back and guided him past fatal feathered shadows. Now his rage has matured into a cool elongated subtlety. During the day his lidless eyes have kept watch for feathered oversized sky chickens with claws and beaks. He's been lucky. Being a ground hugger and perfect camouflager, he's got through the lines and now he's staring at green flesh, a perfect hardon. His fantasy à la carte, ripened pond protomensch, and now he can get even with the Egostist from Eden. If you can't get a human, try a caricature.

Mother flashes through his verdant pond. He loved his mother. His dad was an abstraction.

"Why did you take her?" Herschel sobs, flicking his split personality at the sun. His rage liquefies. There are no window wipers. A discharge, lachrymal gonorrhoea... "Mother... Mother... why?" he hisses in self-hatred.

A dreadful silence pervades. He charges at his own reflection in the water, so much self-hatred fills his conduit ... Mother ... Mother ... he sobs, as only a snake can sob. If he had hands, he'd scrub his eyes out. If he had stubs like Miss Blossoms', he'd scrub his blinkers hollow. The shine of good fortune, however, is not with a lowly landeel.

He turns around the bend. He'll try the crystalline waters, cool his aching belly, and after a while he notices (being a tactile and sensual animal) that with the brisk shock to his system (it cools his rage and focuses his mark) he can think more clearly: A whole new world has opened up because of aqua therapy. Cooled into a new snake, the Mom craving is gone, and his lenses are clear. He bellys over slowly...

Emma had warned Victor to meld into the trees: green on green. "Maybe the dumpy meatloaf is full of flies: that means black caviar, what a treat," slinking Herschel says, ecstatic. Green against grey sand. Fatal. "Love you," hisses Herschel. The straddler lying back in the sun, has enhanced the chromatics of death; Herschel sends out his tongue ... the heated organ expands like a true erection. "I can't believe my luck," hisses Herschel, staring lidless into the sun.

Meanwhile, Emma has taken a powder, evaporatd into the

vegetation: the invisible woman. "I warned him," she cerebrally ovulates. "What a fool he is." She spews out sweet spit at the light waves beaming past her. The light waves form a choreographic outline. Victor is lost in sweetest Oblivion. His brain is eating cosmic chicken while the gastric juices bubble away for fly delight. Glue gurgles out of Herschel's mouth, gastric glue. Sliding into a figure eight, he moves on his noon day luncheon. Glue drips over the straddler, the acidity in the glue kills the straddler's nerve endings under the skin, and therefore, there's no pain, only frost. Victor shivers. The glue is local anaesthetic. Victor yawns and nothing more.

Herschel smiles. His jaw is already over Victor's soft shoulders. The jaw expands like a vise ... the confident mouth sucks the bullfrog in by micro-inches.

It's so damned chilly. Victor awakens with the spittle on his body holding him in position. He has the distinct impression that he is being pulled into a tube, an endless tube at that ... cold ...

Victor shivers. "It's only a dream," he shivers. "IT MUST BE A DREAM."

And he goes on dreaming. Wake up, lover, Emma balloons.

Victor feels so light that if he could only let go, he'd float up from the ground. There are dark raisins up there.

Eddy in the Ice

Eddy, don't screw around with the crystal. Something's holding the whole shit together, all those dark raisins of delight and decay. There's glue out there. Most of what's out there is space. We're separations ... we are foreign matter ... iron ... phosphorus ... calcium ... breaking down and glutinous, ... a hell of a lot of water, too ... breaking that down into space ... A dreadful silence pervades, held in an unseen embrace ... You see, Eddy, you're part of the imploding glow, baby, part of the lachrymal snow ... a regular ice worm ... swimming in an icefloe ...

The Meat Freezer

A few hoods hit a local butcher, Manny diSokoloff, to settle accounts because he screwed them on a drug deal. They muscle the available patrons and Manny into a freezer. The dead have closed lips. "Look, you guys," a hood says. "I got nothing against you. Believe me, this aint personal, so turn around and face the meat."

"Give me a break, boys," the manager shouts into the foggy dew.

"Shut your mouth, Jackoff," a hood called Snakeyes says. The manager gets on his knees, pleading for his life while the meek patrons face the immense slabs of meat suspended from steel inverted question marks.

A shot, followed by an explosion. Blood trickling down to the human bowling pins on the concrete floor. Snakeyes walks around pumping a shot into each head, neatly between their eyes.

"I need an Eno," Snakeyes says.

The next morning, the headline in the Toronto *Telegram* said: WE NEED A NEW POLICE CHIEF.

The hoods are clean as they leave the freezer, not a print on the meat of the door handle.

My memories are hung in a deep freezer. They carry my prints. A few have been snuffed but most show their faces. Surprisingly, they all have white gloved hands, as if touching the living were to risk infections. How many stiffs are hanging in somebody's freezer? Is there a memory in your meat freezer? Has your pal been missing for a month? "TURN AND FACE THE MEAT. DON'T ANYONE MOVE," the man who will leave no prints cackles. It's Eddy, and there's dry ice on his elbows. The concrete floor is covered with brown bullies popping their carapaces. Manna for Manny and other moochers who thought Minnie Mouse had tits and were titillated by the unreal promises of a life beyond the butcher shop.

Miss Orchard

Her stiletto heels touched the ground, moving like robin's legs. She wore a tight checkered skirt. She moved to chalk out a sentence on the board and her buttocks complemented the ripple of her hips, narrow as they were, suggesting a slight elevation to the lustful eye. How can I describe the emerging animal heat she inspired in me? A chemical heat, some inner-glow caused me to raise my eyes in the same way a bird watcher does, afraid of flushing a rare fledgling. A faint shadow-line of cleavage accentuated by a smart silken blouse, her breasts were petite sweetness ... I hovered like a bumblebee before breaking into a chapel of dusty hollyhock. I might have been an insect resting below her white throat to hear molecules singing forth from Miss Orchard ... I could have been ...

Her mouth was a redish pink, not quite a salmon color, but one chromatic shade less, and as she smiled her teeth revealed touches of nicotine discoloration, jarring the symmetry of her clean white skin, face and throat, and a slender white hand whose finger nails glowed from fresh nail polish: but her fingers were also tainted with nicotine, brown blotches under a coating of white from the blackboard as she brushed away the white pollen and shook the chalk dust loose. She formed a sweet kiss, blowing dust away from her mouth, and charisma followed her like a noon day shadow. Even her soft cough and the nectar rattling in her throat took on mystical meaning: both goddess and imperfect human, slender nymph cultivating tubercules. The woman brightened my general day of depression and gloominess. Ever conscious that the students knew of her tobacco addiction, she kept staring at her hands and then quicky corrected her gaze and stared at us. Her tapered legs trembled.

She drew her forefinger across her lower lip, repressing a painful shyness, a vulnerability. Her hand moved to support her chin while she tried to bend our concentration, her eyes two blue aquatic creatures on the rim of a calm lake, eyes sometimes grey, sometimes glowing when angry. If a dim-witted student caused her to lose the handle, she exploded in a puff. A sharp rebuke, a verbal stab, and then nothing more. The calm lake. Two creatures on the run. Her facial armor left the impression a light-weight moth leaves on a nocturnal bloom a little after sundown. She puckered her lips, they nibbled at an imaginary gerund. Puckered lips, a full oval face, dark red brownish hair (she may have been a redhead), cheeks rouged and the cheek bones sharp, so that the living doll's face was dispelled, the dreaminess gone. No matter how she scrubbed her hands the stain was there, her teeth weren't snowing. Her smile became tighter. She placed a hand over her mouth, then drew it away. A half-blown kiss. The stain of half-life to come.

Miss Orchard never threatened. A sharp rebuke and it was over. But how many would have gone to their psychic deaths just to have their hands examined by her before due punishment? Not a hint of violence, and no fix from the Good Book either. Kids made her nervous, the lascivious wet lower lip of some moron peeling her in his mind's vacancy down to the bone, but what really worried her was a morbid fear of a dangling participle, a screwed up phrase, a sick gerund in need of repair. She hated a misuse of decorous adjectives and recommended that we memorize new words; our vocabulary greened all the more. An increased vocabulary was a leaf absorbing sunlight, increasing its sugars and goodly nourishment down to the roots. She drew a sketch of a sexy plant dining out on sunlight. She sent arrows depicting atomic particles across the blackboard. I followed her gyrating hips as she moved with the solar waves. She hated grammatical deviations and the misuse of adverbs. Hatred sent a twist of nervous energy, her chest swelled, imprisoned birds rose. Some student caused a pulsation of anger and a sunny spot appeared above her cleavage, a rash on that delicate white skin which appeared all the paler. Sometimes her whole face bloomed and when the flesh cooled, it had the whiteness of lily.

I became convinced I had powers of invisibility. I could indulge my voyeurism. My peepers were my friends. I sent them out silently to explore Miss Orchard's grammatical structure. I loved the way her lips pursed while forming the letter "O" – and her captive breasts swelled, her throat bubbled. My lights must have shone ... I drew up a poorly constructed sentence. She raised her eyebrows in disbelief, and then suddenly ordered me to wash my hands. I still don't know what hand-washing had to do with a misconstrued sentence, but I hastened to the sink tucked inside a closet and immediately soaped my hands in green strong soap. I detected urine in the sink; some maleovolent punk had peed on the soap; my hands began to smart and burn. I marched back into the classroom and presented my hands to Miss Orchard. She became alarmed. We both marched to the sink and she said very little but carried an embarrassed expression. I sat silently in the classroom, gazing down at the floor. From time to time, she looked in my direction and back to others in the room. She tried reading signs of guilt on the faces, but if she suspected who the rascal was she said nothing. Miss Orchard kept referring to her book as though it contained secrets from beyond the crypt. Some unsaid shame hung in the air. My hands had broken out into a furious rash. My fingers began to itch. I imagined they were scalded butterflies. I wanted ice to cool the fever. I let my eyes rove along the rim of her face; by this diversion I hoped to forget skin eruptions.

    I should have listened more to her love of language but she was also there to extend my visual vocabulary. She flowed in black high-heeled shoes, my eyes climbed her legs, my eyebrows brushed back her dress, they ached to see delicate frilled panties. She had drifted to my desk and in a dignified voice whispered that I had best cool my chapped hands under the cold water faucet. She drifted back to her desk where she locked one leg over the other, for she sensed carnality. She warned the class that the sink was out of bounds. Carnality was out of bounds. Cool the hands in the closet of corruption. Leave no particle dangling in a world in which endings never agree. But somebody had left a polished apple on Miss Orchard's polished desk. It sat there. Impossible to avoid. The apple had a wide ass and a double sheen. A solitary leaf hung from the centre core; a slightly green protuberance, a wee leaf. She gazed lovingly at it, and smiled to complement the robustness and rotundity. She appeared sweet as that very ripened apple. She stared directly at us. She had our eyes, heart and ears. She stood up, her two lovely arms swaying. Her long arms, her nails polished; I think of flowers. The bell rang. We filed out of the room, single file.

The Lake

A powerful wind whips over Eagle Lake causing chops of water to lick through bays and inlets. The moaning and writhing along the shore, an aquatic dirge. Fed by a chain of neighboring lakes and rivers, the waters of Eagle Lake are chilling with eerie currents at different depths, so that even in July it seems some wild joker is dropping ice cubes into the drink. The black water connotes a sunless freezer; only the hardiest of fish survive.

At mid-lake the water is deeper, darker and colder, the light lost with each layer of icy water. It's as if a glimmer from a small pen-light had forced its way through an inkwell. The depth at the centre strikes the imagination; you begin to think you are privileged to be at the point where several ounces of lead and fishing line keep falling until you yawn or think the line has struck bottom, but then there is a sudden jerk and the line continues to fall. Everybody loves to brag about their favorite lake, and as it happens, it is the deepest lake on the planet and usually a northern lake, a forlorn lake, ignored.

At the dark centre, I kept hoping my fishing line would disappear into another dimension, an aquatic twilight zone where one meets souls of the departed. That notion tickled the fancy of a fourteen-year-old: the lake of death; and maybe some hand would surface with a mighty sword ... or at very least, a prehistoric monster, half fish and part beaver would surface to see who the violators of the sacred silence could be. And were there swimmers foolish enough to go skinny-dipping in the frigid soup? I like to think I was the first person who saw a giant squid glide past a canoe in that lake. Perhaps sunlight played against the surface of the water, distorting anything that passed my view, but I had seen the *thing* and I didn't press the point, fearing ridicule. I didn't mention garfish or a creature with an elongated serrated narrow mouth lurking in the coldest depths; it wasn't a good idea to float about on the darkest water.

An aquatic mood, as opposed to a human one, a minnow or a pod of minnows, are cells skittering like thoughts below the lips on the body of water. I thought of minnows as flecks of thought pursued by heavier thoughts in a chain of cannibalistic renewal: the smaller diminish, the larger fatten. The losers, those slow dim-witted life forms – minnows – are soon devoured, and others who are sick, too weak, or who can't adapt to a more rigid existence, vanish, food stock to larger fish thoughts. The result of this purge – not a molecule of fat wasted. No fat floats around the heart of the lake, and sometimes if one listens to a dreadful silence, you are conscious of the pulsating beat as the canoe is swept to one side or the other.

I believe poetry is often revealed in the evening, at midnight on a day in July. I am staring at the expensive crystal-ware in the sky, and see bits and pieces of silver fall toward the lake; fireflies sizzle and dissolve. It's dry ice, splinters and shards of frozen carbon dioxide at absolute zero ... falling into black water, devoured ... a soul becomes gas ... I see the lake as a body in deep sleep; the bed in which that body turns is a basin and denotes the outline of a bowl composed of volcanic matter, igneous buckshot from the explosion at birth ... a basaltic bowl filled with bone-chilling tears and restless fish population, or impulsive thoughts. Collectively, they form a conduit, or psychic telephone line to the other world above the surface of the lake, or the dream outside the dream where somebody answers all unrecorded messages. My thoughts fall into the water and if I concentrate on just one pore on the surface, somebody or something will answer. A silence forms a skin over the lake, not a ripple or breeze present. The surface is glassy. The lake is pretending to be dead but I don't trust the lake. The lake can think, it absorbs thoughts because it stores energy from sunlight, from fish life, motion in the currents, from thought. The lake is breathing, filaments of thought move through its entire system, and then that brain explodes. The water heaves, picking up momentum, inhaling, exhaling ...

The light dims in the sky and the lake appears dark and brooding before a summer storm and that mood moves like a viscous substance filling up the eyeball of its own sadness; and then the sky allows a sheath of light to touch the water and sunlight ripens, not at the centre of the lake, but closer into the shore before the water darkens and you are aware that the light has gone into the *drop*, and from the drop the whole widens and falls further into some psychic abyss where fingers of currents drag the luminescence down and devour it. Near the shoreline, the water is transparent, not a residue of impurity there, no foreign matter, and an illusion takes hold. The swimmer feels that he or she is above the purest substance on the planet, resting on a liquid eyeball and staring directly through to the pebbles at the bottom. You could stare forty or fifty feet down and pretend you are resting on a magnifying glass. You can see every pore, every detail, a sunbeam of fish darting behind a rock formation. The creature dissolves inside a private condominium. A few bits and pieces of gravel go up in its wake and then fall. There is so much clarity here you begin to feel that any light ray would instantly cauterize the slightest contamination. A few miniscule strands of algae fall away, burnt by a light beam ... or has a goldfish nibbled at it? A dark sliver flees across the floor and I wonder how that sliver of intelligence can flee from joy.

The sun is warming my body. I do a dead man's float face down, hands in front, feet straight as a log ... and soon my skin begins to itch from the heat of the sun. I dive as deep as I can, pushing a fluttering sunfish out of my way, but dive as I may, I still can't match the magnificent penetration of a sunfish jabbing through the water, having its fun, or sex, with the elements. A cold current catches the roof of my spine and I strike up to the surface with the cold trailing me. I'm stabbed by an invisible finger of ice. No wonder minnows enjoy this form of coitus with mother water. I watch them thrive around the current. It revitalizes them. Born again minnows. I realize how they feel when they are sent into exile, into the holding tanks of Uncle Nathan's fish emporium. Fresh Fish. They craved and worshipped that cold current, one of many deities in the poltergeist establishment. How painfully lonely they must have felt in Nathan's limbo, his fish tanks, and what a poor substitute that cold water proved ... that man-made current ... not enough vigor to wash away the staleness of their spiritual decay. And soon they'd be united with a stronger current in a darker world. But in the midst of my dark forebodings I have this sensation: either I or the lake is a bulbous dream, a see-through dream, and both of us are trying to empty ourselves of all thought. The lake forces out its minnows, I expel my thoughts. Boo, I cry, blowing bubbles at golden hordes. Boo, they reply, before they evaporate into the cold deep ink.

Moose Call:
On a Tree Frog is a Unit of the Universe

The lean garter snake with its longitudinal stripes fell into a deep sleep, stroked and massaged, and then he was offered a tiny tree frog by Moose, a wiry juvenile delinquent who shared our cabin at summer camp, a boy who wore his name like a trooper and who had acquired a streak of creative sadism. He was expert in wrist burns, hot foots, toothpaste sandwiches, and snakes in your bed. He glowered all the time, but not at his serpent who snored softly. The snake opened its mouth, yawning, or it had a subtle case of hiccups. Moose smiled and yawned, too.

Moose could turn anybody into a peanut, staring directly with fire in his eyes, and at the slightest flicker of reproach he would shout, "Who are you looking at ... Maggot breath ... huh?"

"At a moth, honest, it flew by ... honest Moose ..."

Moose hocked a goober at the kid's white runners. "There's your moth, dummy." He burst into deranged laughter, the laughter of the abyss, or some hole where bears shit in the woods ... His insane laughter infected the cabin. Moose rarely washed; he was as aquaphobic as a long-haired Angora cat.

Some among the cabin dwellers tried to neutralize his animal musk with a pine spray, and braver boys opened windows here and there to create a breeze effect. They applied themselves to purification when Moose turned his back, but soon the mug suspected a change in the atmosphere; the lout enjoyed a hot house environment, heat and sweat, especially his own (a ripened pair of sneakers inspired his nostrils ... socks ... decay and sweat) and soon he snapped with indignation. "What's that smell," he roared at the nearest kid, who backed away in terror. "What's that shit I smell?" The kid played dumb and shook his head.

"That's just fresh air, Moose."

Moose concluded he was having a hallucination.

"Hey, you," Moose shouted at the smallest kid in the group.

"Huh, you mean me," the boy replied.

"Yes, you," Moose replied, squeezing the kid's elbow. "Give me a deuce or I'll deck you."

The frightened boy offered his oppressor a few crumpled bills, his dad's allowance kept in a deep pants pocket. Moose laughed, unfolding the paper as though it were the petal of a flower. The kid kept muttering about being broke, but not too loud. Moose had mentioned a knuckle sandwich too often: all believed him and filed out of the cabin in silent protest, but I sat on the corner of my bed determined not to give in to Moose's many-tentacled oppressions.

Moose directed his lights on me. "How come you didn't leave with those other jerkoffs, huh?"

I weighed his question carefully. "Cause I don't run out on good company, Moose," I replied politely.

Moose sniffed the offending crisp air drifting in off the lake.

"Close the door would you?" Moose said, an expression of terror in his eyes. "Jeez, you'd think Mother Nature creamed her drawers." And then he added, "You aint a dumbo. You got a good set of lights ..."

"Lights?" I said, puzzled by his cosmic reference.

"Yep," he said. "You're as sharp as my Ralph ..."

Moose called all his pet gartersnakes Ralph. They proved therapeutic to him. They were his companions at summer camp. He confided in them in a hushed tone. He told Ralph all his fears, superstitions, dreams wet or dry. And Ralph, or *Raph* as he was sometimes prone to call his pet, listened like a skilled therapist, demanding only the odd feel, a firm molestation of its belly, and then the snake seemed to smile and this pleased Moose. Ralph was his analyst, mother, father surrogate, his closest pal.

I made a few cerebral notes. Who would believe my Ralph recollections? Who would unglue hyper-reality from a dream state stemming from a rustic world; if you believed in Ralph, then it might be possible to talk about tree spirits and the souls of dying sunfish.

"You like these here land eels?" Ralph asked after a momentary pause. "Yes," I replied, taking care not to appear patronizing. Moose and Ralph hated sentiment. "They sure got some appetite, I'll tell you," Moose continued, in awe of Ralph.

"You're the big star here, Moose," I said. I felt like a psychic detective playing with a dangerous and diseased brain ... everything that pulsated under Moose's dome was fascinating; he confided in snakes, he could have been a synthesized ghoul from the bog ... violence not far from the hair trigger in his paranoid brain ...

"It's boring here except when you feed Ralph," I said. Moose nodded. He hated every social function except archery, when he gawked at the young women instructors. He loved their long narrow legs ... He considered himself a leg fancier. I wondered if he had

Ralph or *Raph* on his mind when he pulled on the bow and the instructor hugged his back and showed him how to draw the string of love. I heard Raph hissing: "She's good for you ... feel her up ... like you touch me ... slowly ... touch their white thighs press your fingers up ..."

"This place stinks," Moose declared. He searched under his bed for Raph who had taken a powder.

I could have told Moose that guys like Raph were a dime a dozen but I might have got a dry knuckle sandwich. After a while, we gave up the search but only after I suggested Raph had gone to empty his bladder. Maybe Raph urinated through a microscopic hole in his striped carpet, or crapped it all through a side door in his skin ...

Moose warmed up: the idea of a snake relieving itself appealed to him. He embarked on the topic of Nature's disposal units, and how important snakes were to the environment, and how they controlled insects and consequently the disease which issued from every bit of vermin that flew. He explained how snakes ate the bugs that eat trees, and then the frogs ... those same amphibians who licked flies ... He intimated a bizarre relationship existed between fly, frog and snake. He licked his lips, referring to the "threesome." "You see, Rosie (he called me Rosie), a frog eats his weight in flymeat, and soon the dummy can't move cause he's eaten all that flyshit ..."

"You mean, a frog is really a pig with a brain in his belly?"

"It doesn't make sense," Moose went on, staring at me with pity. "I mean, who would want to eat a spring peeper loaded with all those buzzin raisins? ... so stinking full a frog can't blow any of his wind ..."

I reflected on this wisdom, which had a jewel inside its shell.

"Did you know a frog is a unit of the universe?" Moose asked.

"A what," I muttered, sure he hadn't dropped that gem.

Moose expanded on the subject, speculating that they came from hyper-space ... a cosmic pond ... He stabbed his finger at the ceiling. He spoke about rain, and storms, of horrendous water spouts in the sea, and how furious forces scooped up straddlers ...

"Did you know that they came with the rain. Sure, you see pollywogs or something like them in dirty water, but they're not *real* frogs, not like the ones that fall from the sky. There's water, yes, Rosie, pure water, and frogs swim in the sky ..."

I listened carefully. Moose deliberated on the secret life of the frog and how they fucked around in the sky, and how they humped each other's back ... how froglings broke from the skin of their backs ... Moose wasn't just any nutbar. He was pure Hershey with nuts in his head, cashews, macadamians ... He appealed to my curiosity like a rotting mushroom, a leper, a crook, a sword swallower ... and he insisted the sky pond wasn't conventional soup like you'd find on earth, not like potato soup. Moose's soup had its origin in nebulous gases. Was Moose talking about Chick's favorite topic (after Isaiah), *dryice*? A pond of dry ice in the sky. He was happily alive in his psychic pupa, drawing wierd and wonderful utterances past their elastic limit into the humming space of metaphor ... He was the unsprung poet ... and I wasn't about to inform him that he would surely end up in a straightjacket kicking the rubbery surfaces of a rubber apartment. He was a rare wild one. He had swamp fire in his eyes.

"I'm telling you," he exhorted, "that every frog is a blessed unit..." Triumph bloomed on his face.

"Blessed," I said, unable to contain my surprise. "If they're so damned blessed, how come they get shot down your pal's tube?"

Moose reeled. Logic stung him like a stinger in his brain ... A horrible silence crept over him. He paled. Was he going to rip my head off and then shit in it? But his eyes mellowed. I had put out the swamp fire. He appeared genuinely hurt, but no rage surfaced. My barb was nothing more or less than a sliver of doubt. Finally, a sentence rolled off his lip, a hurt sentence.

"I saw them fall from the sky," he said, and then closed like a butterclam at low tide. He had admitted the unthinkable. He looked quickly around the cabin. Panic prodded him. "You didn't hear me say that..." He had the vision of a rubber room, a man in a white suit explaining to his mother that her son would never ever be a chartered accountant. He started searching for Ralph. "Falling from the sky..." He ducked his head under each bed. "It's Moosie calling ... come on Raph ... come on little fellow ... pretty Raphie ... here Raphie ..."

"Try some milk ... snakes love their milk ..." I assured him, and then slipped out of the cabin, marching away from the main path, but Moose never followed, though I heard his voice trailing off somewhere like a wounded animal. Later in the evening he was seen beaming his flashlight at the base of a tree. I never asked if he found his tubular friend.

He became more reclusive, convinced that everybody knew his darkest secret. When hunger forced him to make an appearance in the dining hall, he kept his distance, turning away from everybody; the food, he quickly plunged into his mouth. Camp songs repelled him. He hated joy. Solitude yearned in his damaged soul and so he looked out on the lake each evening. Bats swooped down into the branches and frogs sang around the bend of the Oblong River tonguing its way into the lake. They ballooned their praises of Moose, who hummed along, longing to join their chorus and club.

I tried to decipher his epiglotal sounds, but couldn't. Moonlight turned Moose's features into a sepulchral mask and as the light dimmed his face, his voice sank deeper into his chest. He melted into the woods, calmed by its skin of darkness.

On the third Sunday, somebody said that Moose had left with his mother.

"Why?" I asked.

"Who gives a shit," a boy replied, "the jerk is gone." He said that Moose had gone for a dip, but not in the lake.

"You mean, a breakdown?"

A few kids shook their heads. "Maybe, who cares?" They all loathed Moose, pinched for a deuce or two, remembering their chafed wrists after Moose gave them a burn, or his hot foots. Moose had roared mightily into his frog pond, the sky.

But now Moose had left with his mother. She had pushed him into a Buick, but not before slapping him across the face and shouting that he was rotten, rotten as ... she kept repeating, purging herself ...

"Rotten as what?" I said. She had called Moose an abortion. An aborted unit in the universe.

I asked about Ralph. Nobody cared. There were too many Ralphs creeping around the woods. Nobody had seen him clutching Ralph when his mother pushed his ass into the car, and there was no Ralph left behind in the cookie box ... So Ralph had taken a powder and vanished, too. Ralph and Moose, gone.

"What did his mother look like?" I asked a witness to Moose's abduction.

"Kind of funny," the kid replied. "Her legs were small" ... and he looked frightened. "She looked a little like a frog," and for some reason the kid began to sob.

Dream Frost

Creativity begins in the invention of disguises: a tiny green tree frog like a shift of light on a leaf; a toad reclined against the trunk of a dead tree, the rough skin blending with the bark, mottled leaves and roots ... power of instant invisibility. There's no where to hide. You stand perfectly still, concentrate on being part of the background. You pretend to be the bark of a tree, a leaf on a bough ... endless possibilities. I've imagined myself as a toad being absorbed by forces in the tree, or the ghosts, if it is a very dead tree. I feel rootlets running into my arms ... suddenly so damned radiant ... I'm an oily wet creature: a slimy frog fresh from the mill pond ... glue trickles out of my skin ... a speckled pond fly is stuck on my skin. I feel its pressure ... trying to free itself ... it sings a brittle lullaby ...

    The kid with the nervous bladder was sleeping in Crunchdale's class. Crunchdale didn't hear the kid's soft snore. Somewhere in his memory a garter snake yawned. He ignored the snake and the snore; both became invisible. But the kid dissolved in his seat; pee was running down the aisle and this time, even a flatnosed-bullet personality like Crunchdale could neither ignore the smell nor the trickling across the dusty wood floor on a warm spring day. He opened the window. This did little to lessen the odor. He opened several windows. The kid with the bad bladder became invisible. He continued on with his lecture. There wasn't a problem, the breeze was mugging the piss on the polished floor. The school janitor would have to mop up his own reality. Crunchdale orbited about the room, worried. The bladdered kid was snoring loudly. The little garter snake showed his snout through the memory curtains. Crunchdale pressed a fresh handkerchief over his mouth to keep the smell out. The bullet turned a pale pastel pink. He shoved a hand through a hole in space, gently pulled the kid's head to one side and the snore was dulled. The snake was gone. Nobody had said boo. The class was silent as an icicle hanging from a wintry roof.

    The child with the magic bladder disappeared into his chair. Maybe he was never there? The urine inched toward the front of the classroom. Sunlight poured over the trickle turning the piss a translucent yellow. It was a streak of sunlight, radiant. I heard a child singing a brittle lullaby. Crunchdale smiled, standing there all in sunlight.

Time in the Buff

Sorting out marbles in the buff, it beamed on my battery cells that sensual femaleness, the nude, was subdued throughout my halcyon days. Summer camp lectures on sex tended to play down the sensual and spiritual chemistry of the sexual act; the tone was venerably clinical, overly polite as a camp nurse held up a chart of the male and female anatomies and tootled in a cool voice about the tributaries to the testes: a matronly woman councellor giggled in her nervousness and pointed to another anatomical portion, that so-called "safe" place, the brain ...

A male councellor reminded the kids that rutting led to larger complications than pregnancy and a ruined life for both rutters: VD and then insanity, blindness, and eventually an excruciating death when your codpiece fell off and down into a dank sewer. You ended up pissing sulphuric acid, your appendix the root of black rot as boilings spread to the rest of your body. The cure? A hot needle inserted into your penis, the cure worse than the disease. The hot needle attacking the infected area *deep* in your water-supply hose; and nobody wasted super star penicillin on a sex maniac when it could be used on heroes just back from the war. Abstinence helped, and playing with one's self, although frowned upon, was acceptable, but only as the last lugubrious choice. The chief honcho laughed and put his hand back in his pocket. A few kids gasped. Was he going to play pocket pool?

What about love? Some rutter popped the question. If boy and girl were in love would it then be safe and acceptable? Did love lead to blindness? The head honcha, a lady with golden hair and freckles, proved sympathetic to the kid's anxiety attack. Although the act couldn't be officially sanctioned, she said, nevertherless it did happen as a prelude to marriage and babies. Pregnancy. The honcha showed what sperm could do ("show us your stuff kid") and how it led to fertilization. She seemed to enjoy eggs floating up the canal. Motherhood, the batteries sparkled. Sanctioned sperm out on a blind date with an egg. The honcho agreed. So there we were, trapped. Heat in our system and what to do? It led to the sulphur pits either way. What to do? The honcha suggested we sublimate our drives. Go and read a good book, go swimming to cool out. Shower. The shower was all too often the final solution. We tried saltpetre. There was no controlling nocturnal emissions. I dread the wet dream.

Moose had never turned up at the sex lectures. He had played with the frogs. He had told me how they humped each other, how they gave birth from their backs, how the skin broke and the froglets leaped out. Moose had laughed. I hope he's made it across his mother's pond. Too bad, though, missing those lectures. The lady councellor and her small pointed breasts. Did I crane my neck, staring up her legs? Guilt has put a patch over my eyes. Heat cooled the venereal bug. I thought about trees, and later I filled with water the prophylactics Moose had handed out. We threw water bombs around the cabin. They didn't explode, they bounced like mad molecules. The image of Moose's mind.

Rutting, mothers, frog love, molecules, tubercules, mirth. Mirth in the woods, in the form of George Formby; in flight from Moose and the tubercules of sex, I remembered Formby, a wartime British comedian-singer who played on his banjo and strummed wildly with his shrill voice racing ahead of the vibrative steel banjo, which was his alter ego and constant companion. It grew on his body, it became a sex symbol, and the way he strummed it made Jimmy the Cricket seem to be crossing a club foot with a thighbone. Consider this: Jimmy the Cricket as Caliban. Anyway, everybody loved George, including Rebbe Noble – who excused me from after-school Hebrew class in the Fall of 45 when he read my anxieties. Formby strummed joy to the civilized world, even if his sounds were tinny. George was a proto-type wimp, because he seemed always wanting to please the proletarian tea and biscuit crowd; and sometimes he strummed up the social ladder to royalty. Working women loved him as they polished up assembly line bombs. He strummed his head off, a short man, almost anorexic, his voice oily and far too sweet. But how that banjo rang while Hitler was pulling Europe's stomach out through her cultured asshole and Moose watched frogs falling from the sky, and there I was, begging Rebbe Noble to be excused so I could see my hero on the silver screen ... beam on his large front teeth ... and I recall getting some wax buck teeth so I could be just like George ... teeth that were sold along with candy cigarettes ... I sent garlands of garlic out to his soul, to his rodentic expression, and blew him wax kisses just as the diva of the chlorinated deep with her Nereid lips and empyrean voice rose ... Esther Williams ... out of endless pools, the still pools of sensuality ... the mirror image of Moose's ponds...

I melted into the plush observing that beautiful human goldfish ... what a woman, swelling in her bathing suit until I ached to find out what femininity really was like beneath that horridly tight fabric. She didn't give an inch of buff away. She made concealment an erotic form. She sang in shimmering olympic-sized pools, a melodic gush while doing an effortless breast stroke, projecting a blithe spririt, bubbling in effervescent glee, a manic up-and-down minnow in bent space. All the incredible orchestration of concealment, and I could hardly conceal my longing, my chompers clamped shut on Formby's wax teeth, twanging away.

For relief, there was *Hoppy* and his friends (his real name was Wm. Boyd), Hopalong Cassidy ... a macho grey-haired cowboy all in black with a tall white hat (twenty gallons to cover all that integrity), and a mean long silver gun with a pearl handle. There were no notches in his handle, unlike the dirty bushwackers waiting for him behind a cactus. Hoppy looked like a retired steamfitter, and spoke like choked steam: very slowly ... "ah wouldn't ... go for that ... iron, Mister ..." and yet he killed with the speed of a blink in time, and I loved how he outgunned some dusty whippersnapper of a thug on the dry street, blowing the dipstick right to the Great Dipper, and then Hoppy flipped his gun back into his shiny dark holster, adjusting his flashy gun belt, adjusting his tall hat, apologizing to his horse or some lady for the momentary blurr of violence, the adjustment from life to death for some punk. It was loony, to a sagebrush tune, but the real prize for lunacy went to lusty Lassie, noble canine and royal bitch ... always in the buff. How bright she was ... I remember a sunny spring day in the early forties when our school turned out with Union Jacks fluttering (talk about Imperial idiocy) to meet that bitch in her shiny light brown and white coat, her narrow head and ears perked up ... her tongue lapping, and the press of a hundred kids shouting ... all loving Lassie who had found her way home, no matter where she found herself, no matter how far away, how abandoned ... and she could count ... just like Trigger, Roy Rogers' horse ... and her coat glistened, sanitized, and her smiling long puppyish tongue hung out to our hearts ... her coat cultured in the Outer Hebrides ... what an innocent ... she barked for us ... Hip Hip for Lassie ... Hip Hip ... Lassie, somewhere in hyper-space, munching artificial dry-iced dog food ... At least you didn't get stuffed like Trigger, who was my kind of horse.

Another smiling prairie crime fighter, Roy ... the puppy of the cowboys, a song or a prayer on his lips ... a silken outfit ... a good gun belt ... nice holster, and the shooting iron silver as a tea tray ... a long thin barrel as skinny as Roy ... Hoppy took his killing seriously. Roy did more singing than killing and did a lot more riding ... He and Trigger ... with Trigger white all over and tall and healthy as any Horse should be, and clean as Hoppy's hat. Trigger could count with his leg, he could count to ten, but could he do fractions? ... did he read Roy's lips? ... Did he have sex? Did Roy? No. Serenity was in the six-gun and the song.

The cactus popped some blooms into the cool desert night. Purple blooms. Somewhere bushwackers were moving in on cows ... rustling ... Hoppy would find the grizzly saddle-suckers ... "Draw ..." Hoppy always gave the sucker a break, and then popped him with his clean shooter ... "Damn fool," Hoppy said, going through swinging doors into infinity ...

A pellet whistled past my face. Some bushwacker is blazing away at me. It's either an air pistol or a bee bee gun. It could have split my eyeball like a grape. Hoppy would have cornered the disease and wasted him. Under the influence of Errol Flynn, I swung at my pal Harvey Schwartz. I liked to swing at Harvey. Sometimes I tried to pigstick him with a broken broom stick ... down the lane ... a little way from a swampy chasm, a flooded hole that was an abandoned building site. There, one balmy spring day, I was pigsticking Harvey toward the abyss. I hoped to pigstick him into the swamp ... but I caught him on the saddle of his nose and it bled profusely. It didn't stop bleeding. It gushed. I ran into the house and got some ice. Harvey had a shocked glassy stare. "You did it ... You did it ..." His eyes were intact. "You did this to me ... I thought you were kidding," he said. "You rat ..." Harvey bled, but later he smiled and it made me feel better to see him shine on my victory ...

Why was Harvey smiling like a hyena? He even shook my hand to show there were no hard feelings. "How about some boxing?" he said. Well, I owed it to Harvey. After all, pigsticking had been my choice. How could I turn down a boxing match? If Harvey boxed as badly as he pigsticked, I would cream him with a few vicious jabs. I turned up honorably on Sunday. Harvey had a pair of bulbous gloves for me. I searched Harvey's gloves for any iron. The gloves were hard as Crunchdale's leathery soul. It occurred to me that Harvey's gangly long arms might have the zap to render me senseless. Harvey joked about canaries whistling up a song for the loser in the basement rec room. Harvey, thin as a bean pole and taller, had long legs. I knew I had to work quickly into his mid-section and slug him down to the ground.

"So," said Harvey, backing off in a leggy, dandy movement. "Go ... go," he laughed. He proved quicker with the jabs. I remember hitting the canvas, and a rush of bird song. I tried getting up; I had no feet, there was no ground. Harvey swung a dispatching *coup de grace*, and another thump. I collapsed in a rush of nausea and vertigo. Harvey smiled. The smile had a sickening shine, and Harvey beamed it for my sake. Blood gushed out of my nostrils. Harvey slammed my ear with his deadly mitts. Good measure, and then the other ear. As long as I attempted to get up, he'd punch me into a state of disrepair. "Stay down, damn," Harvey shouted. Blood kept flooding my nostrils and Harvey went to get ice. He applied a large handkerchief of ice to my forehead. I didn't know which was worse, the cold that numbed me or the nausea or the humiliation of defeat. I never took Harvey up on the offer of scientific boxing again. I preferred the pigstick, but not Harvey. We were even. Although Harvey carried a scar across the saddle of his nose. I rode him for life.

Time in the buff. Neighborhoods change. A house is repainted, the buff is hidden. Moose is gone. Harvey is gone, too. Rumor had it that he got some woman pregnant and blew in his noodle. There were those who believed, even as children, in the blown-in noodle. Like Larry Weinburger, master of the well-stocked goober ... who always complained, "You're living off the fat of the land, and believe me, you peckerhead, you'll pay for it ... go ahead and laugh ... you slug ... you're no damned good ... your old man is killing himself climbing ladders ... painting houses ... and what are you doing ... yeah ... I'm speaking to you, jackoff ... don't laugh ..." A goober struck the stairs of his house. Oh, he was expert in goobers. It amazed me how sadness glistened in his huge eyeballs. Then, hock. He had a penchant for the phrase "fat of the land" ... and I represented sloth and other valences of indolence.

Larry's real distinction, however, was that he lived next door to a gorgeous dwarf lady who brought the hots out of me. She glittered, compact, with pointy tits, a narrow neck, and shapely round hips. She wore a short dress to bring her leginess out, legs which were evenly tapered in her nylons, and the black spiky shoes emphasized her legs, especially when she moved her perfect buttocks around, slowly shifting or seeming to rotate with the movement of her hips. She was a blond. Her hair swam back to the small of her back as she glided with her tapping narrow black shoes, black as Captain Midnight. Her eyes were deep blue. She had an oval face, certainly not wide, and she knew how to please when she applied pinkish red lipstick to her small mouth; and I wondered how she sustained herself. Did she eat her meals in tiny sections? Did she love tiny men? Did she take them in tiny sections? A powerful scent of lilies whiffed to my senses. Flowers of the dead, or resurrection?

"I suppose you're coming in your pants, you creep," Larry whined, with venom in his oily voice. "I bet you'd like to fill her little crack," he slobbered, and his eyes came alive like sharks in the night, though it was daylight.

Sometimes, with her short dress, I saw a frilled panty, a delicate light blue panty with very white lace. The drooler muttered he could see her source ... "I don't believe it," he watered on. A faint ouline of pubic hair tickled the frilled border ... had she tamed her delicately small mound ... shaved it ... I asked Larry what he thought about the shaving. He glared at me and spat another goober. "You're seeing things ... put your eyes back ... go and jerk yer wire ..." And then he burst into a rain burst of cackling laughter.

After that, Larry avoided the topic of the dwarf but I saw him watching her while she took in the sun, reclining on a small wicker chair. She stared up at the sky through sunglasses. She had the shortest pair of shorts I had ever seen. Larry ogled out of his blood-shot eyes. She started stroking her thighs, stretching her white legs until they seemed to grow a few inches. She rubbed her thighs up and down, brushing and pressing her crotch. She kept glancing in his direction, shifting her buttock to rub her other thigh, and as she rubbed, her cheeks bounced. She had drawn a tube from her handbag and squeezing, she proceeded to rub lotion in the palm of her hand. Now, she forced the cream the full length of each leg, straining until a button fell away on her blouse and a small breast bounced out. Larry strained his eyeballs. She pursed her lips as she stroked her thighs after the oiling.

Larry spat a vicious goober past me, and then one rolled off a dewlapped lip. His huge bug eyes filled with mist, and the coats of flesh which hung over his wide distorted jaw expanded in rage. "Listen, jackoff, the next fuck you get will be your first ... you bird brain ... no woman will give you a piece ... you'll pay a whooore ... shit face." He spluttered and emphasized SHIT FACE, and it gave him pleasure to repeat it. His anger and frustration increased his watering, huge molecules dropping out of his mouth. I decided to take a walk. I feared his terrible spit. I dreaded the wet dream. It was clear to me: Larry was doomed to live the wet dream. She had become invisible for him. He had driven her back by sheer will power until she became smaller, like a bee backing into a snapdragon, and then he felt safe and quietly enraged, until after a while he forgot why ... and knew only the rage, which was as relentless as his drool.

In His Bandages, The Poet

A 1936 flick. Claude Raines played his first film role, but it was all done in bandages. In fact, nobody got to see his face: it was either bandages or a blank space. Had he been zapped by a death ray? The protagonist was removing surgical dressing skilfully wrapped about his head. The bandages filled out a human form and this had kept the poor vaporized fellow from going off the deep end. As long as he had his bandages he could delude himself into believing he'd be his old self again. He was doing a slow strip tease. The *Invisible Man* shuffled about the lab in his kimono and slippers. *Get those rags off*, I cried. The worm of curiosity got the better of his invisible soul. He stopped making psychic love to himself. He started breathing heavily behind the gauze. he was done with his substitute skin, that vibrative outline. His breathing became asthmatic hisses and guttural noises behind the dressing. His lips vibrated. Panic seized him. He tore at his dressings, pulling them until the tail end of the wrapping was removed. A primal shriek followed. It reverberated throughout the theatre. The experiment to restore his former self had failed. He held up a mirror with a high micro polish. Nothing existed from his neck up, not even an egg plant ...

In his grief, the Invisible Man failed to see that those surgical dressings had given him the thing he didn't have before: character. He was too wrapped up in his ego to realize that he had had an *average face*, but the gauze had given him individuality, an intensity equal to any monster's power. I was compelled by him, titillated as I watched the white pickers of his glove seizing a match ... I craved to see the lighted cigarette dangling from his invisible lips, the invisible man headless, the audience mindless, addicted to his suffering. I laughed along with the crowd, my sides bursting from an ingrown raillery, and a few snobs actually sniggered at the sight of the Invisible Man's fedora floating above his neck. Sometimes, the freak wrapped a silken scarf about his face, and somehow it covered his invisible mouth up to the saddle of his invisible nose, and if you looked carefully you could detect a void where his forehead resided.

This gave that fedora prominence. Out on the street late in the evening, the fog gave the impression that it was slowly devouring him, leaving that fedora for the last, until it too drowned in the foggy dew of other scientific souls who had given thir best shot for science and were zapped by an invisible ray, a black light beam, or a vaporous bolt of lightning ... crazy gas ...

Years later, I am haunted by my monsters but not nearly so tormented as that bandaged martyr to scientific probings. In a smoggy dream, I shuffle through a narrow street and coming toward me is the poet, none other than the Invisible Man, but he's not wearing his usual gift wrappings. The faithful fedora is resting on his head like a sacred church dome. A thought flits across my mind: how does he clean his teeth? Does he gouge the nylon brush into that slit of his bandaged face? But he isn't wearing his bandages, he's sporting his favorite scarf. He raises a tightly bandaged hand, forcing a picker in my direction. The finger trembles. I suspect he is suffering from an invisible hangover.

"You're gone," he rasps maliciously, his veil shaking. I now suspect he is grinning. I hear a bubble of laughter caught in the drain of his thoat.

I begin to strip away my skin.